CW01456013

Babies Come from Glasgow

An exploration of love and loss in my family

Carol Ann Morison

Grosvenor House
Publishing Limited

All rights reserved
Copyright © Carol Ann Morison, 2025

The right of Carol Ann Morison to be identified as the author of this
work has been asserted in accordance with Section 78
of the Copyright, Designs and Patents Act 1988

The book cover is copyright to Carol Ann Morison
Cover design by Brian Jones

This book is published by
Grosvenor House Publishing Ltd
Link House
140 The Broadway, Tolworth, Surrey, KT6 7HT.
www.grosvenorhousepublishing.co.uk

This book is sold subject to the conditions that it shall not, by way of
trade or otherwise, be lent, resold, hired out or otherwise circulated
without the author's or publisher's prior consent in any form of
binding or cover other than that in which it is published and
without a similar condition including this condition being
imposed on the subsequent purchaser.

A CIP record for this book
is available from the British Library

ISBN 978-1-83615-109-8
eBook ISBN 978-1-83615-110-4

In loving memory of Rody, Kath, Helen, and Glenn.

The information in this memoir is based on my personal recollections and perceptions, my sincerest apologies if any details are not 100% accurate or are incorrect.

Introduction

Grimsby
February 2009

Although I was expecting the call, the shrill ringing phone startled me. I took a deep breath and lifted the phone from its cradle next to the bread bin on the beige tiled workshop. I always made, or took, significant phone calls standing up – not sure why but maybe it made me feel more assertive. I glanced over my shoulder. Glenn had taken my place at the table, and although he had looked apprehensive all morning, he gave me a reassuring nod.

I pressed the green button on the ringing phone, my heart beating so loudly it was echoing in my ears and threatening to drown out any conversation.

I cleared my throat and said, "Hello."

"Carol?"

"Yes, is that William?"

"Aye, but my friends call me Billy."

The strong Glaswegian accent surprised me because I knew he had left Scotland in the early 1970s.

"I wasn't sure if you would sound Scottish or Australian but it's clear you've never lost your accent," I commented and smiled though he couldn't see me.

"We were wondering if you would have a Scottish or an English accent – you sound English." Billy sounded surprised.

"That's probably because my accent was never strong to start with and I moved to England nearly 40 years ago."

I heard a voice in the background with a distinctive Australian twang.

"Tommy is asking which football team you support, Carol?"

"Celtic," I replied quickly.

"That's great, so do I," Billy confirmed, "but unfortunately Tommy supports Rangers!" I heard a 'huh' in the background and assumed it came from Tommy.

"I guess having lived in England since 1970, you may have expected me to say a team like Manchester United or Chelsea, but my dad supported Rangers, and I remember teasing him at the start of the 1966-1967 football season by saying that I was going to support Celtic. When they won the European Cup in 1967, I was hooked for life." I paused for a few seconds before asking, "Who did Helen support?"

"She was Celtic too. Tommy's the odd one out," Billy replied.

I heard whispering in the background, this time it sounded like a female voice. "Who else is with you, Billy, apart from Tommy?"

"Barbara and Linda."

I knew that Barbara was William-now-Billy's wife, that Linda was Billy's sister and my half-sister. Billy and Tommy were both my half-brothers.

At the age of 54, I was finally speaking with members of my birth family who although they had not been aware of my existence until a few weeks earlier, sounded pleased to hear about me. It was like one of my childhood dreams, growing up as an only child longing desperately for siblings, had finally come to fruition. I turned round to Glenn with a huge smile on my face, but he just looked worried.

At that moment I knew I had to meet them face to face even although there were more than 10,000 miles between us!

Chapter 1

Where babies come from

When I was a little girl, Daddy told me several times over the years about how he and Mammy had gone to Glasgow to choose a baby. He explained that they had seen lots of babies lying in cots but when he looked in my cot, I put my hand up. I suppose it must have seemed to him that I was saying 'choose me' and that's exactly what they did. So, in my childhood innocence Glasgow was where babies came from. The actual word 'adopted' was not used until much later, but by then it did not come as a great shock.

However, my childish naivety about where babies came from caused me to argue with my friend, Jane Stevens, who lived across the road in a cul-de-sac off our main road, Kennedy Terrace. Jane was nine years old and small with brown curly hair and freckles. Her family had come to Stornoway a few years earlier when her father took up the position as manager of Lipton's grocery store on the corner of Church Street and Cromwell Street. It was the school summer holidays, and we had started playing 'houses' in the open porch of my family's pebble-dashed council house and were using our childhood imaginations to make it up as we went along. She had a big crush on Cliff Richard after seeing him in *Summer Holiday* at our local playhouse on Beach Street in Stornoway, so she was pretending to be Mrs Richard and was making his tea of chips and beans. Not to be outdone, I piped up that I was married to Dr Kildare, star of the same named television series that I watched avidly every week. I thought Dr Kildare was very good-looking in his white clinical coat and I had decided I didn't like Dr Gillespie because he often criticised the enthusiastic and well-meaning junior doctor. Of course, neither I nor the world had any inkling about the actor Richard Chamberlain's sexuality at that time.

I fetched two of my dolls, Sally and Rosemary, down from my bedroom, two blankets from my doll's pram under the stairs and two spoons from the kitchen and we pretended they were our babies. Sally was supposed to have ginger hair, but I had become a bit over enthusiastic one day when I was playing hairdressers, so she was almost bald with just a few remaining wisps of orange nylon poking out of some of the little holes in her head. As Jane was my guest, I kept Sally and gave her Rosemary who had a luxuriant head of curly blond nylon. We rocked them and fed them imaginary food on the spoons, stopping to wipe up the imaginary food drips and burp them regularly. Jane was very good at making a baby crying sound from her throat but when I tried it hurt so Sally turned out to be a very good baby.

During one point in the game, Jane took one of the blankets, folded it, pushed it up under her tee-shirt and said, "I'm going to have another baby." I looked at her because I didn't know what she meant. She could see that I was puzzled. "Don't you know that babies grow in mummies' tummies and then come out of their bottom?" Jane was a year older than me and she knew an awful lot. I was usually impressed but this time I was horrified, you poohed out of your bottom!

"That's not true, babies come from Glasgow. You're a big fat liar, Jane Stevens."

We argued and both ended up in tears. Jane ran home to her house across the road, and I ran into my house. Mammy, who was in the kitchenette ironing (it must have been a Tuesday), asked what was wrong. After I told her she sat me down on the settee and explained that she and Daddy had not been able to have a baby of their own and that I had been chosen and adopted by them which made me very special. She also confirmed that babies do grow in mummies' tummies, and I had come from Glasgow because that was the city where I was born and where they had adopted me. I was very confused, had I been in someone's tummy and if I had, where was that tummy now? I still had images of babies covered in poo, but I was soon distracted when Mammy asked if I wanted a glass of cream soda.

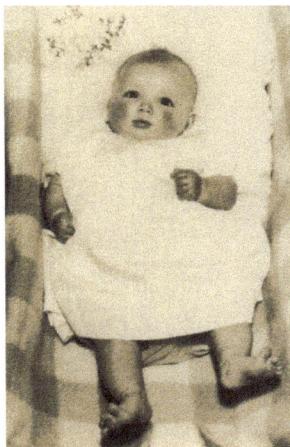

This Baby came from Glasgow in November 1954,
aged four months.

Chapter 2

Daddy and his family

Daddy's name was Roderick Adam Hunter Morison. His father had been called Roderick Adam, and I had gained the impression growing up that the name Hunter was after a minister at Martin's Memorial Church. However, more recently, *Ancestry.com* showed that his paternal great-grandmother's family name was Hunter, so I guess I'll never know the actual source. All the family and his friends called him Rody but to me he was just Daddy. Mammy's full name was Kathleen, but everyone called her Kath apart from her mother, my Grandma Trowell, who called her by her full Christian name.

I have some recollections of Mammy when I was growing up, but I have far more mental pictures and memories of Daddy. Looking back now I can see that Daddy's life had a particular rhythm to it, comprised of a series of regular repetitive rituals. One was winding up the big wooden arched clock that sat on the sideboard at around 8:00pm every Saturday night, another was preparing the food for our Sunday dinner on Saturday afternoon. Maybe the repetition is why I can recall him so clearly or maybe it was because I felt closer to him than Mammy.

Daddy used to leave for work before I left for school, and he always smelled of shaving soap when he bent down to give me a kiss on the cheek. On Saturdays I sometimes sat on the bathroom stool watching him mix the shaving soap in a bowl and spread it over his face and neck with the brush he took from a small stand on the window ledge. I was fascinated by the way he swept the razor up in straight lines ploughing through the soap like a spade through snow. Just occasionally he would catch his skin, mutter, and stick a small piece of Izal toilet paper on the nick to stem the bleeding. Izal paper was not very absorbent, but it seemed to do the trick because he never left the house with bits of paper on his face.

On Mondays on the way home from work, he would call in at Campbell's newsagents on Cromwell Street and collect *The Sunday Post* and my *Diana* comic. The Sunday papers always arrived on the Monday morning plane because there were no flights onto the island on Sundays or shops open. Sunday was the day of rest and anything that could distract Stornowegians from praising God and resting on the Sabbath was prohibited. Even the swings in the three play parks in the town were padlocked on Saturday evening and not released until Monday morning.

After tea on Mondays, Daddy would read *The Sunday Post*, and I would read my *Diana* comic sitting next to him on the settee. When I had finished my comic, he would pass me the centre pages of *The Sunday Post* containing the strip cartoons of 'The Broons' (The Brown family) and 'Oor Wullie'. Poor Wullie with his spikey hair always seemed to be getting into trouble as a result of mischief or mishap. On Thursdays, Daddy would go to the newsagents again and bring home the *Stornoway Gazette*, our local weekly paper, along with my *Judy* comic and again we would sit together on the settee and read after tea.

He always made me feel special and I have lots of photos of the two of us together in various locations, on beaches on Lewis, in Edinburgh, in the garden, on the settee together, etc. There were very few photos of the three of us together. The only decent one, meaning a photo with no heads partly chopped off, that comes to mind is a black and white professionally taken photo that sat in a lime green frame on the top of the bookcase in the living room. In the photo my parents are standing on either side of me, and I must have been standing on something because our heads are at a similar level. Daddy is wearing his black suit jacket and a pale shirt with a striped tie and Mammy is in what looks like a plain black dress, but may have been any other dark colour, and a string of pearls. I am chubby with a round face and a mass of Shirley Temple curls in a halo around my head. I don't know how old I was, but I could have been somewhere between 15 and 18 months. Daddy was about five-foot-eight, he had bright blue eyes and

Daddy, Mammy and me.

dark hair until it started to go grey. He always combed his hair back from his face with a wet comb and then created a slight centre parting. Sometimes when I watch films of James Stewart, particularly in later roles like Charlie Anderson in *Shenadoah*, the actor reminds me of him, more because of his manner than his looks.

Daddy wore shirts with separate collars attached to the shirts by tiny brass studs that he kept in a round shiny brown box that sat on top of the tallboy in their bedroom. The box had a section in the centre for the studs and the collars were placed around it. He wore cufflinks, a tie clip, braces on his trousers and sports jackets with leather patches on the elbows for work, topped off with his grey gaberdine coat and grey felt trilby in cold weather. His out of work clothing was similar but the shirts were collarless, and he wore plain-coloured woolly jumpers. In my mind's eye I picture him in a grey one. Sometimes on holiday he wore a green flannel shirt with short sleeves. He only had one suit, a black one, which served a dual purpose as he wore it to formal dinners and funerals.

One photo of me as a two-year-old that I always liked shows me sitting on a doorstep with Daddy's pipe in my mouth, unfortunately it was taken with an old folding Brownie camera and the top of the picture has a broad white band across it where the negative had been exposed to light. I remember watching him over the years preparing his pipe, one of his evening rituals. He would sit in his usual seat after tea and use a pipe cleaner to gather the remnants of the burnt tobacco out of the pipe. He would lean over and tap the pipe on the inside of the fireplace twice to empty it and then carefully fill the bowl of the pipe with fresh tobacco taken from a brown leather pouch and tamp it down with his forefinger. Lighting it with his silver petrol lighter always seemed a challenge as he would puff and suck on it for several minutes until the tobacco finally caught fire and sweet-smelling smoke would fill my nostrils.

In the living room we had a three-piece suite, in brown fabric with a randomly scattered faint pink flower pattern. The settee was positioned up against the wall separating the living room from our small kitchenette and was at a right angle to the fireplace. Daddy always sat in the right-hand corner of settee and there was a small narrow table beside his left arm where he kept his pipe and tobacco. One chair was positioned to the right-hand side of the fireplace facing the settee and that was Mammy's chair, and the second chair faced the fireplace. I would often sit on the settee leaning against Daddy in the evenings, feeling the heat from the coal fire and watching black and white programmes on the small television standing on spindly legs in the opposite corner. Pipes went out of fashion so as an adult I rarely came across someone smoking a pipe but when I occasionally did, the smell immediately took me back there to evenings sitting beside Daddy in our living room.

One Saturday morning after Daddy and I had been to Charley Barley's butcher shop on Manor Park to buy the meat for Sunday dinner, another weekly ritual, we walked into town to Woolworths, the biggest shop in the town, and he bought me a small pink plastic clock with a knob on the top that you twisted to move the hands round. When we got home, he taught me to tell the time. It was also Daddy who taught me how to tie the laces on my shiny black school shoes.

* * *

One of Daddy's daily routines before breakfast was cleaning cinders and ash out of the nondescript 1950s-style beige tiled fireplace in our living room. He put two sheets of newspaper onto the hearth, lifted the larger cinders out of the fire grate with a shovel repeatedly until there was a little mound on the newspaper and then he scraped out the smaller cinder bits and ash that had fallen below the grate tray with a poker. The final stage was to brush out the residual dust, fold the newspaper and carry it carefully through the kitchenette, before depositing it in the dustbin outside. Then he rolled up more newspaper sheets into long tubes and folded them over his hand several times to make spills, placed them in the grate and liberally loaded pieces of coal on top of them. The fire was then ready to be lit later in the day during weekdays. Sometimes it was lit earlier at weekends, particularly in winter.

Every Tuesday the noisy coal lorry would pull up outside our house and the coalman came down our path with a dirty hessian sack full of coal on his back that he dumped noisily in the metal coal bunker in the back garden. He was covered in coal dust; it was on his clothes, his face, and hands. I remember he always wore a black beret, but it may not have started off life that colour.

I suppose I grew up in a smoky atmosphere, but I wasn't aware of it at the time. The living room was not big, and the air must have been heavy with the fused emissions from Daddy's pipe, the Capstan cigarettes he occasionally smoked, Mammy's Embassy tipped cigarettes, and the coal fire. There was no central heating in Stornoway in those days and an island off the north-west coast of Scotland is closer to Iceland than Spain, so I felt cold for most of the year apart from the odd day in summer. This was not helped by Mammy's insistence on opening the sash windows in every room each day, leaving a gap of four inches 'to let some fresh air in', even in winter – and it was certainly fresh. I loved to sit in front of the fire, absorbing the heat and watching the flames flick up towards the chimney and look for patterns and shapes in the burning coals and flames. If I sat too close, I got the red mottling on my legs that we called 'Tinkers' Tartan'. A steel companion stand sat to the right of the hearth with a small shovel, tongs, a brush, and a toasting fork all precariously perched on its hooks. Sometimes in winter Daddy would place slices of pan bread on the toasting fork one at a time and we watched the bread slowly turn golden brown from the heat of the fire, somehow that toast always tasted better than toast from the grill on our gas cooker.

Although we burned coal, many households in the town and on the island burned peat. Lewis and Harris have extensive heathered moorland with peat bogs underneath. Writers believe that they were formed between 3,000 and 4,000 years ago and some have speculated that the peat bogs on Lewis go down as far as 20 feet below the moors. In ancient times the island would have been covered in dense woodland which eventually died, and the decomposing vegetation was preserved and formed peat.

As you drive around Lewis you can see the dark brown peat banks cut into the moorland like rows and rows of one-sided trenches. I used to think that they looked like an enormous version of a Lyons Jamaican ginger cake that had been hacked into.

Getting peat from the peat bank to the fire involved hard manual work. First, peat slabs needed to be cut from the peat bank with a peat iron called a tairgear in Gaelic. Then they were laid out in a certain way on the top of the bank to allow them to dry. When they were dry enough, they were transferred to a lorry and driven to the house or croft where they would be burned as fuel. Transferring them from the lorry to the area where the peat stack would be located was a 'many hands make light work' job. I recall on some summer evenings standing in a chain of our neighbours which stretched from the lorry to the peat stack, passing basket creels full of peat from person to person along the chain. I didn't mind being part of that physical process, but dry peat is very dusty and if a wind was blowing, I would often get peat dust in my eyes, and it stung.

* * *

My paternal grandmother, Agnes Morison, lived with Daddy's sister, Auntie Agnes, at Woodside, 34 Scotland Street, Stornoway. Woodside seemed huge compared to our small two bedroomed semi-detached council house. It had a formidable appearance from the outside, granite with white-framed sash windows, a low wall with spiky green railings on top at the front of the house and a high wall at the back. At the side, there were two outhouses converted from the original stables. Grandma Morison

Me with Daddy on the day of Grandma's funeral.

died at the age of 80 on 20th August 1959 exactly one month after my fifth birthday and I have a photo of Daddy and myself taken on our settee on the day of the funeral.

In the photo he is wearing his black suit, white shirt and tie and a very serious expression. I am in a sleeveless blue dress clutching one of my dolls, she was called Catherine. I had thought that Daddy was born at Woodside on 13th May 1909, but recently I obtained a copy of his birth certificate, and it cites the birthplace as being 20 James Street. When I saw it, I had a vague memory of Daddy saying they used to live on James

Street. Daddy and Auntie Agnes had an older brother called George, who apparently developed a drink problem as a young man, an affliction that was not unusual on the island. The family took money that had been saved up to send Daddy to India (I never found out what he wanted to do there) and shipped the embarrassing older son out to Port Elizabeth in South Africa in the 1930s. He never returned to Stornoway and died out there in the 1980s. Daddy hardly ever mentioned his distant brother, but I know that Auntie Agnes and George wrote to each other from time to time because she told me.

Daddy and Mammy met during the war. He was in the RAF; she was in the ATS, and they met each other in the small Scottish town of Strathpeffer which is 20 miles north-west of Inverness. After marrying in Hull in January 1946, Mammy and Daddy moved into Woodside with Grandma Morison and Auntie Agnes but as the latter could not help interfering in everything, they decided to move out of his family home long before they adopted me. The council housing list was the only option at the time as it was a static housing market and there was no new private house construction. Initially they lived in a first floor flat at 16 Torquil Terrace but when I was young, not even one year old, we moved to 41 Kennedy Terrace where I grew up and lived until four days before my 16th birthday.

Inside Woodside, the large hall was dark with a door on the left to the dining/living room used every day. To the right, there was a sitting room reserved for special occasions or respected visitors, a piano sat in there, proudly but silently. Ahead, an elegant staircase wound up and came back round on itself, halfway up was a stained-glass window with a red central glass panel and a purple glass border. I often went up these stairs to the bathroom and looked down on the walled garden at the back of the house, distorted and red. The house always smelt of disinfectant.

I have a formal photo of Grandma and Grandad Morison on their wedding day, apparently taken in a studio in Glasgow.

Grandma and Grandad Morison on their wedding day.

The only other photograph I have of Grandma is one taken in her back garden with Daddy, Auntie Agnes, and me as a baby. She is tiny, slightly hunched over at the shoulder and sitting back on her heels looking at me. Daddy and Auntie Agnes are kneeling more upright, and he has his hands behind my shoulders propping me up. Auntie Agnes is the only one looking at the camera which presumably was being held by Mammy. Daddy had slightly hunched shoulders too which became more hunched over the years maybe because of working at a desk every day in the Labour Exchange, a forerunner of the Jobcentre. In the photo, Grandma is wearing a black dress with a white collar, her snowy white hair drawn off her face and tied in a bun, a quizzical expression on her face. I vaguely remember seeing her small and pale, lying in bed in the bedroom that overlooked Matheson Road but like the photograph, it is a static image. I cannot remember her moving, talking, laughing, or smiling.

Me with Grandma Morison, Daddy and Auntie Agnes.

Daddy didn't talk much about Grandma after she died; Auntie Agnes was the more usual topic in our house as she was a strong character with many opinions and there was always a bit of tension when she was around, more on Mammy's part than Daddy's. A few years after Grandma Morison's death, I saw a photograph of her flower-covered grave taken on the day of the funeral. She is buried in the Morison family plot in Sandwick Road Cemetery beside my grandfather, Roderick Adam Morison, who died on 23rd July 1943 at the age of 68. On Lewis, when a married woman is buried, her maiden name is the one inscribed on her gravestone. As Grandma's maiden name was also Morison with one 'r', the name on her gravestone reflects both her maiden and married names. Morrison is usually spelt with a double 'rr'. The Morisons with one 'r' are supposed to have originated in the Port of Ness at the Butt of Lewis. It was probably either an older version of the name 'son of Moris' or the result of a spelling error, but whatever the source it was a pain in the backside for me. When asked my name for official reasons it was "Carol without an 'e', Ann without an 'e' and Morison with one 'r'." What a mouthful!

Daddy told me once that a new-born baby is also buried in the family plot. She only lived for half an hour, and they called her Kathleen after Mammy but there is no mention of her on the headstone. The cemetery has a high red wall around it and rolls gently down towards the sea, a beautiful view the residents cannot appreciate but soothing for visitors. I remember a large white church opposite for the villagers of Sandwick, but when I visited Lewis in 2021 it was not there anymore although there was a modern-looking church further down the same road. When I was growing up there were nine churches in the town of Stornoway, three were Church of Scotland, two Free Presbyterian, one Seceders High Church, one Episcopalian, one Catholic and one Plymouth Brethren, not to mention the Kingdom Hall of the Jehovah's Witnesses on Church Street, ironically.

The Seceders Church was opposite Woodside, where Auntie Agnes continued to live after Grandma Morison's death. On Sundays they held three long services there, morning, afternoon, and evening. There was no melodious organ accompanying joyful hymns of praise, only mournful psalms in Gaelic led by a type of cantor. Mammy and I always went to Woodside after church and Sunday school, dressed in our Sunday best, me in one double-breasted blue coat after another and Mammy in one of her best two-piece suits with a matching hat, and we sat in the living/dining room drinking milky sugary coffee and eating digestive biscuits. The dirge from the Seceders across the street was the backing track to our mundane conversation. Double glazing had not come to Stornoway yet.

On other days, Auntie Agnes' house was always deathly quiet. A silent television and a mute wireless; quite different from the light or home programmes on the radio during the day and television in the evening at home. I always found the silence at Auntie Agnes' house unsettling.

* * *

Auntie Agnes also worked in the Labour Exchange located on Francis Street and apparently, she was a grade higher in the Civil Service than Daddy, but then she had not had to break her service to go to war for six years. About 50 yards further up Francis Street from the Labour Exchange was an empty shop with a central door, two large windows on either side and peeling dull orange paint which Daddy told me had been Grandad Morison's General Grocery Store. Daddy's birth certificate described his father's occupation as a provisions merchant. A lot of people in Stornoway bought items on a tab and paid later but in my grandfather's case some large sums of money were never paid to him, so eventually he closed the shop and retired.

Auntie Agnes always smelt of talcum powder. She wore a lot of loose powder on her face and occasionally a dab of lipstick. Her lips were very thin, and looked wet all the time, I am sure it was not lipstick. She had the same bright blue eyes as Daddy and shortish, thinning permed grey hair. She always wore hats and although she took her coat off when she came to visit us, she always kept her hat on. She wore expensive and good quality clothes bought from Inverness or Jenners in Edinburgh, either in person or over the phone. We did not have a phone in our house, but Auntie Agnes did. She was very generous and often gave me money and gifts but then it was almost as if she thought that by giving me things, she had the right to say what I should or should not do. She was always comparing me to other girls in the town, a favourite was Catherine McCuish, a minster's daughter. Catherine was tiny and had short straight black hair which was very shiny and behaved itself all the time. I had thick, curly, and unruly hair which quite frankly often looked a mess because it had a mind of its own. My hair was always at its best when it was long because the weight helped to control it. I have seen photos of me when I was around three, my hair was long, curly, and looked pretty but getting it

Me at 3 years old.

to that point was clearly a struggle for my parents and even more of a trauma for me.

Every Sunday evening was hair-washing time, and I had to kneel on a stool and lean over the kitchen sink. Mammy had bought a brim that was supposed to keep the water and shampoo out of my eyes, but it failed miserably in its duty. The shampoo always stung my eyes, and I ended screaming and struggling with them both as they tried to hold me down and complete the hair washing marathon. Eventually Mammy gave up and took me to Jessie's Hairdressers on the corner of Bayhead and Kenneth Street and had my hair cut short. Without the weight, my hair just went for it. Mammy kept it short and hence the resulting unruliness gave Aunty Agnes the opportunity to compare and comment time after time. In summer 1966, Grandma Trowell was very ill, and Mammy went to Hull to see her. While she was away, Auntie Agnes invited Daddy and I over for Sunday tea. As usual she criticised my hair and Daddy who was a very calm person said to her, "Agnes, if you mention Carol's hair one more time, we will never come back to this house." He had put his normally gentle foot down and I was so happy.

Auntie Agnes had taken the pledge when she was a young woman, so she did not drink alcohol. I wondered if that had something to do with her brother, George, but I never knew. She was also quite religious and apart from going to church on Sunday and having coffee afterwards, would not do anything else on the Sabbath. She had a television that she occasionally watched but it was always off on Sundays. The television in our house was always on and I loved watching Sunday afternoon matinees in black and white like *Wuthering Heights* with Laurence Olivier and Merle Oberon; *Now Voyager* with Bette Davies and Paul Heinrich; *The Flying Dutchman* with James Mason and Ava Gardner; *The Wicked Lady* with Margaret Lockwood and James Mason, and best of all, *It's a Wonderful Life* with James Stewart and Donna Reed which I still watch every Christmas on DVD.

Auntie Agnes was always criticising something or someone and seemed like a very unhappy person. Daddy told me that when she was younger, she had been engaged to a manager at the Labour Exchange who was from Inverness, but he had died of Leukaemia before they got married. My impression of Auntie Agnes changed a bit after that and I felt sorry for her, but I still resented the criticism.

* * *

On Christmas mornings I turned on my bedside lamp and as usual found a stocking at the bottom of the bed and a present from Santa in the middle of the bedroom floor. Unlike the fancy and generously sized Christmas stockings of today, the stocking was literally just a nylon stocking, one of Mammy's. Looking back now it was amazing how much it could hold but I guess that stocking manufacturers had to accommodate ladies with fat legs, although Mammy's were quite slim. There would be some small presents including sweets and these varied from year to year as I grew, but there was always an orange and a half crown coin at the bottom of the stocking. The present from Santa was always unwrapped. One year it was Rosemary, a beautiful doll with blond hair wearing a pink dress and white pants, another year it was a chemistry set. Whatever I had put at the top of my list in my letter to Santa was always there sitting on my bedroom floor early on Christmas morning. The rest of the items on the list were downstairs in the living room wrapped up. It was such a special feeling opening that stocking on Christmas morning by lamp light in my pink themed bedroom.

I always waited until I heard a noise from Mammy and Daddy's room before I went in to show them my present from Santa. Daddy often teased me by saying that when he checked on me before he went to bed on Christmas Eve, I was asleep with one eye open.

On Christmas morning after the paper and ribbon had been put in the bin, I always went next door to see my best friend, Isobel, and we would show each other what we had got from Santa and play with our new presents. It was great fun, and I loved being in Isobel's house with her and her two younger sisters, Catherine and Heather, who were always excited that it was Christmas Day. Then Mammy came for me and the fun of Christmas morning faded as I put on a new dress, white ankle socks and had my hair brushed ferociously to within an inch of its life before we went to meet Auntie Agnes. One Christmas, Isobel, her sister, Catherine, and I were playing with a compendium of games, a present they had opened that morning, and I was really frustrated that I had to leave because I was winning at tiddlywinks.

I don't know if Mammy and Daddy did not know how to prepare Christmas Day fayre or if they didn't want to hurt Auntie Agnes' feelings, but we never had a traditional Christmas Dinner at home. We would go to either the Crown Hotel overlooking the inner harbour or the County Hotel on Francis Street to have Christmas dinner with Auntie Agnes who was always there before us, sitting at the table with her hat on. She always booked the meal and insisted on paying. Sitting to attention in front of the starched white tablecloth with a full place setting of cutlery and glassware, I missed the warmth and fun of Isobel's house. I was also wary of the serious-looking waiters in their black suits with their white shirts and black bow ties and the waitresses in their black dresses, white aprons, and frilly white hats and worried about dripping food or gravy onto the tablecloth which inevitably happened. There was little conversation, and it was an uncomfortable experience that I knew would be repeated for many Christmases to come.

When Daddy, Mammy and I went home after Christmas dinner, the day became special again. We used to watch the Christmas pantomime on television and the latest Brian Rix farce, which was always full of funny misunderstandings and the standard feature of opening and closing doors adding near misses and amusing complexity to whichever underlying domestic narrative was in place that year.

* * *

When I was nine, Daddy or Mammy, I cannot remember which one, told me that Auntie Agnes was engaged and was going to get married the following July. That was a huge surprise to me. She had met a widower called Donald Mackenzie who was usually referred to as DW because William was his middle name, and he had an elder brother also called Donald who they called Dolly. I thought it was very odd for two children in the same family to have the same name. What struck me when I met him for the first time was that he had a very kind double-chinned face and a gentle voice with the intonation of someone who had grown up in a country village where Gaelic was the first language spoken. Uncle Donald, as he became known to me, was a very gentle, relaxed and tolerant man, making him a perfect foil for Auntie Agnes who was much more intense. Uncle Donald held strong Christian beliefs. He was an elder at the high church where the minister was Mr MacCuish (Catherine's father) and he was also involved in the Sunday school there. His first marriage had been childless and as Auntie Agnes was 49 years of age when they married, the second one was too. That was a shame because I think he would have made a good father. When we were out somewhere with Auntie Agnes and Uncle Donald, everyone seemed to know him. This was probably due to a combination of his role in the high church and his job as he managed the Prudential Insurance Company in Stornoway and spent a lot of time driving around the island meeting clients.

The wedding plans started early the following year, and Auntie Agnes took Mammy and me to Inverness to buy a trousseau for herself and outfits for Mammy and myself. As the wedding would take place in July, I chose a sleeveless white dress with horizontal gold stripes, a white band of a hat that curved over the top of my head, short white gloves and white sandals. Auntie Agnes paid for my dress and for the two outfits Mammy chose. One of those was very glamorous; it was a yellow patterned sheath dress with a light chiffon coat in the same pattern and a lovely yellow hat. The other was a pale plain green two-piece suit with a patterned green sleeveless blouse and a matching green hat. Auntie Agnes bought four outfits because she wanted some new clothes for her honeymoon. My favourite was a self-coloured deep emerald dress and coat ensemble with a matching hat, but she said that was for the honeymoon, not the wedding.

The wedding was held in Inverness, and we all flew there from Stornoway Airport. It was the first time I had ever been on an aeroplane, and I was fascinated when we rose above the clouds, and it looked as though we were floating above a sea of cotton wool. Auntie Agnes had chosen to get married in Inverness as opposed to Stornoway because Daddy and Auntie Agnes had a cousin, Ian Montgomery, who was the minister at the Queen Street Church in Inverness, and he performed the marriage ceremony, his older brother Kenneth, also a minister, was present too. The Queen Street title was a legacy from the past as it was actually located on Huntly Place on the bank of the River Ness. It was renamed Inverness Trinity Church in 1977 because three separate churches had combined over the years. I visited Inverness in 2021 and looked for the church on the bank of the river with its distinctive set of steps leading up to the front door and was sad to see that it had become a funeral parlour.

The day before the wedding, Mammy, Auntie Agnes, and I went to the hairdressers and the most significant outcome of that was that Mammy's grey hair became very dark again like it was in the photos of her when she was younger. There was a rehearsal at the church later that day and someone took a photo of Uncle Donald and Daddy outside the church. They looked very serious as if they were going to a funeral rather than a wedding and that photo proved to be a source of amusement for some time to come. On the day of wedding itself we went to Ian's church in big cars. I was in the same car as Mammy and Uncle Donald's sister, Cathy, following Daddy and Auntie Agnes who were in the lead car. Mammy looked very pretty in her yellow outfit with her new dark hair. She thought it was a temporary colour she could wash out, but it turned out to be a permanent colour and she was very concerned about what people would think when she returned to Stornoway with dyed hair. I have a black and white photograph of Auntie Agnes, Daddy, Cathy, and me climbing up the steps obviously taken by the photographer standing at the church entrance.

I don't remember much about the wedding itself apart from walking down the aisle behind Auntie Agnes and Daddy wearing my new dress, hat, and gloves, holding a little posy of flowers.

Afterwards we stood on the church steps for a long time while lots of photographs were taken. Uncle Donald's two brothers, Dolly and Iain, were there along with two of his sisters, Cathy and Teen-Ann. At the

Auntie Agnes' Wedding Day.
Front Row Left to Right: Dolly, Me, Uncle Donald,
Auntie Agnes, Ian, Cathy, Kenneth.
Back Row Left to Right: Iain, Mammy, Daddy, Teen-Ann.

reception held in the Columba Hotel where we were staying, the guests drank Champagne while Auntie Agnes, Uncle Donald and I drank orange juice. I quickly got bored, then Auntie Joyce performed one of her amusing monologues and had everyone in stitches.

After she married Uncle Donald, Auntie Agnes stopped working and started going to the high church with Uncle Donald, rather than Martin's Memorial, our family church. Mammy and I still went round for coffee after church and Sunday school because all the Church of Scotland churches had the same service times. Approximately 15 minutes before the services started you heard each church's bells ringing out all with different tones. St Columba's started first followed by Martin's Memorial and finally the high church. Even as a child, I thought it was a lovely sound.

Auntie Agnes used a lot of sentences starting, "Carol, you should..." and "Carol, you haven't..." I would always say 'no' to the latter even if I had, just to keep the peace.

One of Auntie Agnes' favourite phrases was, "He's a poor soul," referring to any man in the town who was an alcoholic, or "She's a poor soul," when a girl became pregnant outside of marriage. She would shake her head and although it sounded like sympathy, by the way she said it you knew it was more of a judgement. There were more alcoholics than pregnancies out of wedlock in Stornoway, but when it did occasionally occur to an unfortunate girl it was regarded as a sin and frowned upon by the church elders and the establishment.

Chapter 3

Mammy and her family

Although Stornoway and the Isle of Lewis are part of Scotland, the islanders do not have a broad Scottish accent. The way the English Language is spoken has been influenced over the years by Gaelic, the native language of the Outer Hebrides and the Highlands. The main difference is that Gaelic vowels can have both short and long sounds and sometimes the long vowels are applied to English words leading to a slightly different pronunciation, for example the word 'salmon' with a long 'a' sound like 'saamon'. The only consonant affected is 's', particularly if it follows the letter 'r' so the word 'nurse' sounds like 'nursh'.

I realised as a child that Mammy spoke differently to the other people in Stornoway; that was because she was born in Hull on 18th December 1917, the middle of three daughters born to Grace and John Ernest Trowell.

The three sisters were very different. Auntie Doris was the eldest and a nurse who worked in a hospital with patients we would now describe as having severe disabilities; in those days 'handicapped' was the normal description. She was very caring and self-effacing, and had a distinctive deep laugh, thick brown permed hair, brown eyes, a rather large and slightly hooked nose, and I cannot remember her wearing any make-up apart from a dash of lipstick on special occasions. Auntie Joyce was the youngest and the glamour girl of the three sisters. She always wore fashionable clothes, bright red lipstick and kept up with new hairstyles, I remember one summer she had a wide blond streak in the front of her dark hair. One of Auntie Joyce's party pieces was reciting humorous monologues which had her audience rolling with laughter. She was extremely good at it and thankfully she had performed one during Auntie Agnes and Uncle Donald's wedding reception enlivening the rather serious atmosphere in the room.

I have some photos of Mammy as a young woman and she was very attractive despite having a small mole on the left-hand side of her face, close to her mouth. I can remember her regularly cutting the few hairs that grew out of it with nail scissors. Mammy was the cleverest of the three sisters and if she had been born half a century later would probably have gone to university and pursued a successful career of some kind. However, things were different in that era and when she left school at the age of 14 with a school leaving certificate (meaning she had completed a certain level of examinations) she started working in Palmer's Pet Shop on Holderness Road in Hull. I knew that during the war she joined the ATS (Auxiliary Territorial Service) but she never explained what had motivated her to volunteer. Once she told me that she had wanted to drive lorries in the ATS but was not permitted to do so due to her height.

Mammy was tiny, only just five feet. I have photos of her in her ATS uniform and black and white pictures of her when she was younger maybe in her late teens or early 20s and she was very slim. When they adopted me, she was 36 and was not as slim as she had been. Apart from Sundays, she mainly wore twin sets, soft fabric skirts, sensible brogue shoes and wore powder and lipstick when she went out. She always used Ponds Cold Cream on her face before applying powder and I remember her swathing her face in Nivea with its very distinctive smell before she went to bed.

I remember one evening Mammy and Daddy were going to a dinner-dance at the Masonic Hall (Daddy and his father before him were Masons and I still have his tasselled blue satin apron). She had on a short cowl-necked black jumper with three-quarter sleeves, a blue layered long ballerina-style skirt that she had made herself and high heels. She put on a little eye make-up that evening, and she looked very pretty with her black hair curling to just above her shoulder and her big brown eyes emphasised by the eye shadow. Daddy was wearing his black suit with a waistcoat and bow tie. He had a pocket watch chain hanging from the waistcoat and he had shown me the gold Waltham Hunter pocket watch earlier in the evening and told me it was a family heirloom passed down from one generation to the next.

* * *

Mammy and I used to go to Martin's Memorial Church, leaving Daddy to have a lie-in on Sundays. The gothic-style church was built in 1878 and was an imposing building with beautiful stained-glass windows and a very tall spire. The Morison family had their own dedicated pew at the back of the church and each pew could seat up to eight average-sized people. There were four pews in each row and the central two were joined to each other with a walkway separating the central pews from the ones at each side of the church. When I was little, Mammy, Auntie Agnes and I would sit there together. As I got older Mammy joined the church choir and they sat in a raised rectangle of seats just in front of the pulpit with their backs to the congregation. When they stood up to sing, they turned and faced us. Just before the sermon, I and the other children in the Sunday school followed one of the red carpeted walkways down past the choir and the pulpit and went through one of the doors to the dark corridor leading to the church hall where Sunday school took place. The corridor wound round past the vestry, toilet and a small room on the right with stacks of wooden chairs. That room was used for small meetings and on one wall had glass frames with lists of names and dates when children had been baptised. My name was on one of the lists confirming that I was christened in Martin's Memorial in 1955. Sunday school was led by Mr Fraser who taught French in the secondary school, the Nicolson Institute. He was a small thin man with grey hair that was like a tonsure with the front section missing, a bushy grey moustache and he rolled his 'r's. We sang psalms and hymns, prayed, and learned the shorter catechism week after week in that draughty hall. Then maybe twice a year we would get a treat because the wife of the headmaster of the Nicolson Institute, Mrs Addison, who was a missionary, would give us a talk about where she had been. Sometimes she showed us pictures projected onto a white screen and we learned about Tibet and Nepal and the people who lived there.

* * *

When I was seven, a family named Anderson moved to Stornoway and the daughter, Anne, opened a dancing school. Mammy saw it advertised in the *Stornoway Gazette* and took me along to the first lesson. We were told that we would learn ballet, tap, and Highland dancing. I was quite nervous but very excited as I had a book about famous ballerinas including Margot Fonteyn and they looked so graceful in their beautiful costumes. I quickly embraced this new opportunity and attended the dancing school until the Andersons left Stornoway roughly four years later. The dancing school staged a big concert once a year in the Stornoway town hall to show off what we had learned. There was a big dressing room near the stage and some of the older girls helped to put on our stage makeup which gave us greasy orange reflections in the mirrors around the room. Between numbers they also helped us change our outfits. I can remember tap dancing and singing 'On the Good Ship Lollipop' by myself in front of the glaring footlights and at a different concert dancing and singing 'I'm a pink toothbrush, you're a blue toothbrush' with Caroline Silkstone who was a year older than me and lived four doors up the street from me.

I learned the Highland Fling and the Sword Dance, and we would perform these at different venues from time to time and at the Highland games held in the Glen in the summer. Although we practised with wooden swords painted silver, at demonstrations or competitions we used full ceremonial swords with large heads, so you had to jump high to clear them. Once, Caroline Silkstone caught one of the handles with her foot and sprained her ankle badly. I became quite good at Highland dancing and won a competition in the town hall in 1964 where I was presented with a small silver cup. It sat proudly on top of our television set.

Mammy made all my costumes for the concerts using her hand-cranked Singer sewing machine and even made me a brown velvet jacket with lace at the sleeves which I wore with my Morrison tartan kilt, knee socks and pumps at the Highland dancing demonstrations.

An unfortunate consequence of the dancing and singing was that when relatives or Mammy's friends visited, Mammy always pushed me to perform in some way. I suppose she was proud of me, but I did not like the impromptu requests and would sometimes refuse. When I did, Mammy was not happy.

* * *

When I came home from school on wet Mondays, and there were a lot of wet days as the precipitation level in the Outer Hebrides is high, I was always dismayed by the unpleasant smell of wet washing as soon as I opened the front door. After Monday's wash had been boiled in the Hoover twin tub, transferred dripping by a pair of wooden tongs into the spinner and spun noisily for ages, Mammy would hang the items on the pulley above the sink in the kitchenette to dry and I disliked the smell intensely. On reflection I am not sure if it was the actual smell I disliked or the depressing anticipation that one day I would have my own washing day drudgery. Of course, at that time I was unaware of how automatic washing machines would transform that chore to a convenient button-pressing process.

Tuesday was ironing day and when I came home from school I couldn't get into the kitchenette because

Mammy was ironing clothes on the kitchen table on an ironing pad fashioned out of an old blanket and sheet. I used to wonder why couldn't she have done it before I came home or in the living room where there was more space?

Daddy was paid monthly, and he would hand his pay packet over to Mammy who had a series of brown paper envelopes in a shoe box with words on the front like Rent, Electricity, Food, Co-op Savings and she would dole out the money carefully into each of the envelopes and then gave Daddy some back which he put straight into his brown folded wallet. We had a gas meter under the stairs and my parents always ensured that it had a sufficient supply of shilling coins in it to ensure continuity of gas.

Mammy never seemed happy, and thinking about her from my adult perspective, I believe that she was probably homesick. The contrast between the busy, thriving city of Hull, with all its facilities, and this little island in the Atlantic with its narrow-mindedness and unique type of snobbery must have been stark.

* * *

Most summers Mammy and I went to Hull for at least four weeks of the eight-week school summer holidays. Daddy would join us for the last two weeks and the three of us would travel home together.

I was fascinated by Hull with its double decker buses, traffic lights, zebra crossings, fountains, and large department stores like Hammonds, C&A, Thornton Varley, Bladons, etc. When we went to Hammonds, I would make a dash for the strange but exciting moving stairs called escalators and head up to the third floor to explore its extensive toy section; that floor alone was bigger than the whole of Woolworths, the largest shop in Stornoway. I was mesmerised by the rows and rows of shelves with dolls, dolls houses and soft toys. Mammy would get there eventually, and I always got a telling off for leaving her.

I wondered why my grandma, grandad and people in Hull didn't speak like Mammy. They often missed the 'H' off at the beginning of words, so Hull became 'ooll' and hat became 'at'. Other familiar words were pronounced differently: 'snow' became 'snuh' and 'road' became 'ruhd'. I thought it was very funny. Once, years later, I heard a comedian on the television mock the Hull accent. He asked the question, "Does anyone know what a 'fern curl' is? … It's the way people in Hull say, 'phone call'.

I asked Mammy why she didn't speak the same way as the others, and she told me it was because she had passed the entrance exam to Newland High School which was a girls' grammar school in West Hull, and they were taught to pronounce words properly. Newland High School still existed and was probably a 20-minute drive from Grandma's house by car. Mammy told me that she used to cycle there.

Grandma and Grandad's house was quite different from our little council house but not in the same way as Woodside. It was a narrow two-storey, three-bedroomed terraced house with a Victorian bay window to the right of an open porch and it was rented by my grandparents. When you walked through the front door with its maroon cracked paint, you found yourself in a dark entrance passage with a brown painted Lincrusta wall on the left, and two brown doors on the right. The stairs ahead had the same nondescript runner carpet as the hall and the wood on each side of the runner was also brown. The second door on the right led to a room which was the main living area. It housed a red fabric settee, two matching chairs, and a large sideboard with a table in front of it that could be extended. The under-stair area to the left was curtained off and used as a storage area; when I was small, I liked to hide in there.

From the living room you went down one very deep step into the kitchen. There was a single cold water tap with blue tape wrapped around it coming straight out of the facing wall and below it a well-worn Belfast sink. The house had no hot water and a large, heavy kettle had to be heated up on the big old-fashioned gas cooker for personal washing, laundry or washing up. There was a large walk-in larder in the kitchen with a pale green door opposite the sink. It had a strong cheesy smell and the wooden shelves inside contained everything from tins of spam to raw meat and dairy products to vegetables. The oval pale green bowl that we used for washing ourselves was stored on the floor below one of the wide shelves. The décor in the kitchen was in poor repair with cracks in the paintwork and there was an ancient-looking large brownish rush mat on the floor with worn patches and frayed edges.

The backyard was strange and interesting at the same time. As you walked out into it from the kitchen there was a series of outbuildings on the left and a brick wall on the right separating my grandparents' house from their neighbours. At the end of the row of outbuildings was an outside toilet with cracked maroon paint on the outside of the door and green paint on the inside. The building that housed the toilet couldn't have been much more than a yard long and a yard wide, had white-washed brick walls, a standard-sized toilet with a wooden seat and a high cistern. The door could be closed from the inside with a badly fitted hook and eye acting as a latch and you could just see out into the yard through the gap it left. There was no toilet roll, not even the unkind and ineffectual Izal toilet paper we used at home, instead there were torn up squares of newspaper roughly five inches by five inches threaded onto a string loop hanging from a hook on the wall.

Grandma Trowell had a gentle face topped by pure white curly hair which came just below her ear. She was rather rotund and always wore a pinny when she was in the house, even when visitors came, apart from Sundays when she would put on her Sunday best to go to chapel. Grandad had lost most of his hair apart from a rim at the sides and the back, but he had a few sparse hairs on the top of his head, and I can recall sitting on his knee combing them while Mammy helped Grandma with housework. I can picture him sitting in the wooden-armed chair to the left of the tiled fireplace and in front of the only window in the room overlooking the backyard; he always had a packet of Woodbine cigarettes nearby. The top two or three buttons on his collarless shirt were always undone and his white chest hair poked out. Grandad frequently referred to Charlie Peace. He would say things like, "We haven't seen that since Charlie Peace," or "I haven't heard that since Charlie Peace." I thought that maybe Charlie Peace was a friend or a relative, so I was shocked many years later to find he was a burglar and murderer from Sheffield who was hanged in 1879. Although Grandad seemed like an old man to me, he was probably only in his 60s. From old photographs I have of Grandad, Grandma, Auntie Doris and Mammy, I can see that when he was young, he was a very handsome man and Grandma was very slim.

Grandma and Grandad Trowell with
Mammy (left) and Auntie Doris (right).

There was an old-fashioned dolly tub and ringer in the yard and Grandad would help Grandma by turning the ringer handle while she fed the wet items between the rollers. This antiquated undertaking made Mammy's Hoover twin tub operation look positively leading edge!

Then Grandma would hang the washing on a piece of string stretched between a rickety old shed on the left and a hook in the six-foot wall separating their house from their neighbours, Trevor and Irene (pronounced 'Eereenie', she was German). Once when I was still quite young, Granddad rigged up a swing for me and hung it from the door frame of the rickety shed. Mammy had a fit when she saw me on it.

A family called Jackson lived on the other side of the house and I would play with Diane who was about a year younger than me whenever we got the chance. We would often plan little concerts and deliver them to whoever was prepared to suffer, but I can't remember any details. We performed the concerts in Diane's yard because it was bigger than Grandma's and our audience would sit on planks of wood stretched over two upturned metal pails. Diane's mother was overweight and always had her hair scraped back off her face and tied in a short ponytail. She never wore any make up unlike Mammy and I wondered what she would look like if she did and let her hair down.

Grandma and Grandad lived on Leads Road, Stoneferry, an industrial area in East Hull with factories making cement, paint, pigments and crushing seeds to make oils. Before he retired, Grandad had worked for BOCM, British Oil and Cake Mills, on the bank of the River Hull. I never knew what he did there. I read that Hull was the largest seed-crushing city in the world in the 1920s, making products like linseed oil. There was always a pungent chemical smell that hung in the air in Stoneferry, a result of the blended industrial smells.

Grandma was a housewife, but she was very active in the little Stoneferry community. Cousin Grace lived across the road and two of Grandad's brothers, Uncle Billy and Uncle Harry, lived on Glebe Road, which ran behind and parallel to Leads Road, with their wives, Auntie Bertha and Auntie Ellen respectively. Grandad had another brother, Uncle Jimmy, but he lived in Huddersfield, and I only remember seeing him once. Apparently, Grandma had organised and acted in many concerts and plays in the hall of the Methodist church they regularly attended just round the corner on Stoneferry Road. She no longer did this, but the legacy from those times was still there in the small bedroom upstairs at the back of the house. The room was filled with props including hobby horses, clothes, jewellery, hats and sometimes Diane and I used the props in our shows. Also, in that room was a small doll's house with miniature beds, chairs, tables, pots and pans and even little potties to go under the beds. Just like the china ones we used at Grandma's at night. No one wanted to go to the outside toilet during the night and even if you had been prepared to brave it, there was no light in that toilet!

The first door off the entrance passage led to the front room, which was hardly ever used although it was beautifully decorated and had a three-piece suite, in pink damask. There was an elegant tall cast iron fireplace opposite with a colourful tiled hearth where a brass companion set stood to attention. I used to sit at the piano in that room. I couldn't play but liked to press the keys and see if I could get anything tuneful out of it by accident. On the top of the shiny walnut piano stood five photographs in frames. Three were photographs of Mammy and my two aunties with their entourages on their respective wedding days. They were all married during or just after the war and I realised later that the photos were very typical of the period. Mammy's eldest sister, Auntie Doris, had a white dress that was difficult to describe because it was masked by the huge bouquet with trailing ferns she was holding. She had six bridesmaids, including Mammy and Auntie Joyce, and two flower girls. Five of the bridesmaids were holding muffs but Mammy was holding a bunch of flowers so she may have been the chief bridesmaid for the occasion. Her husband, my Uncle Ken, was in full army uniform and his brother, Don, was beside him in a smart suit.

Auntie Joyce's wedding photograph showed her also in a long white lace dress with a veil held back by a pretty, white headdress and Uncle Stanley, who was a pilot, was in his RAF uniform, complete with peaked cap.

In the third photograph Mammy looked very pretty in a white lace dress with buttons down the front, gathered sleeves, a long veil, a spiky white headdress, and a trailing bouquet. Although Daddy had been in the RAF too, he was wearing a dark suit. She had two bridesmaids and a flower girl. One of the bridesmaids was Auntie Doris and I think the other was Shirley Palmer, the daughter of the Palmers who owned the pet shop where Mammy had worked after leaving school. Both Daddy and Grandad were wearing dark suits with turned up trouser cuffs and a handkerchief peeking out of the breast pocket, white shirts and what looked to be grey spotted ties. Uncle Stanley was in his RAF uniform again beside Auntie Joyce in a two-piece suit with a large matching hat perched on top of her head. I assume that Grandma's outfit was fashionable at the time: a long-waisted flowered top over a plain skirt and a hat with an upcurving brim also perched on top of

Daddy and Mammy's Wedding.
Left to Right: Auntie Joyce, Uncle Stanley, Shirley, Daddy,
Mammy, Grandad, Auntie Doris, Grandma.

her head. They all looked so young, but then they would have been.

The fourth photo was of my cousin, Lesley. She was nine years older than me, but in the photo, she looked around three years of age. The fifth photo was of a little boy with blond hair wearing a big smile and a sleeveless fair isle tank top over a shirt and tie. I had been told that he was Auntie Doris and Uncle Ken's little boy Graham who had died from polio when he was six. He would have been my cousin too and I felt sad that I had never met him. Sometimes when we went to Auntie Doris' house, she would let me use Graham's red scooter which was still stored in the garage but neither she nor Uncle Ken ever spoke about him.

I usually saw Lesley a few times during each holiday, and I thought she was very pretty. She was tall and slim with curly dark hair and big brown eyes. She sometimes took me shopping in C&As and afterwards to a café bar called the Pioneer on Jameson Street. It sold freshly made warm sugared doughnuts that arrived on a plate with a paper napkin and fork and although they had an extensive milkshake menu, I always chose the lime one. The café was only a few doors down from Shenkers' curtain shop where Auntie Joyce worked as a secretary and de facto manager so we would go and visit her in her office above the shop that had a full glass wall allowing you to see what was going on below.

I adored Uncle Ken who was married to Mammy's sister, Doris. He was funny and generous. He used to call me Caz and sometimes sent letters to me in Stornoway with photos he had taken of me during the summer holiday. He was slightly overweight, had brown eyes, a thin moustache and dark hair with a side parting. His hair was long on the top and often fell over his eyes if he was looking down. When he was not at work, he favoured cardigans over corduroy trousers and slip-on shoes. He always took us out to places when we were on holiday in Hull in whichever car he had at the time. I remember one that was big and black with a full running board and the inside smelled of old leather and pipe smoke. He took us to the historic town of Beverley on some Saturdays because he and Auntie Doris like to shop for fresh fruit and vegetables at the weekly market. After items had been inspected, selected, and paid for, we would wander round looking at the other stalls overflowing with clothing, shoes, ornaments, furniture, books, sweets, and pictures. Sometimes Mammy would buy cakes or preserves to take back to Grandma. The sun always seemed to be shining when we went to Beverley but on reflection that could have been because Uncle Ken only took us to an open-air market on warm sunny days.

Sometimes he drove us out to the seaside towns of Withernsea, Hornsea or Bridlington where shops on the promenades selling buckets and spades, inflatables, tourist memorabilia, hats, sunglasses, postcards, ice cream, candy floss, hot dogs and the amusements were a novelty for me. I enjoyed jumping up and down on the trampolines and soaring in the air by myself on one seat on the boat swings, but I always wished that I had a sister to sit opposite me on the other seat. The only downside of these trips was that the beaches were very stony and uncomfortable to sit on compared to the beaches on Lewis where soft white sand stretched out for miles alongside the machair (alkaline plains of sandy grass). In Lewis you had to take your own picnic because there were no shops or cafes anywhere near the beautiful beaches in their remote locations.

Every year, Mammy and I would go to Hornsea to stay for a few days mid-week with Grandma's cousin, Lillian, and her husband, Fred, who were both older than Mammy and were retired. We would catch the Number 30 pale blue double decker Kingston upon Hull bus from the bus stop beside Stoneferry Green with its stately Victorian bandstand. I always made a beeline for one of front seats upstairs to enjoy the high-rise journey to the bus station in the city centre. Sometimes as the bus approached Stoneferry Bridge red lights would flash and I was thrilled to watch the bridge separate in two with each side rising high to allow a large vessel to pass by going either upstream or downstream on the River Hull.

Paragon train station was beside the central bus station, so we walked through the diesel fog, crossed the road dodging in between the endless onslaught of buses and taxis and boarded the train to Hornsea. That trainline was one of the casualties of the controversial Beeching Report and closed in 1963, but I can remember travelling on it during several different holidays before it closed. Once it had, we had to get on a dark blue East Yorkshire double decker bus in the bus station and that was a much longer journey than the train ride.

Lillian and Fred lived at 2 Carlton Avenue in a large three bedroomed house with two reception rooms, a breakfast room, and a small kitchen. Lillian had snow white hair wound into a bun at the back of her head. At night she let it down and plaited it – the plait almost reached her waist. She was clearly the boss of the house and Fred generally did not say a lot. I think he had some heart problems, and I can't remember him being very active while we stayed with them.

Mammy and I used to walk from there to the beach or go round the small number of shops in the centre and behave like the tourists we were. I found out many years later that my husband, Glenn, grew up just around the corner from Carlton Avenue in a house on Cliff Road. He was five years older than me, and it is crazy to think that during one of these visits we may have walked past each other not knowing what destiny had in store for us.

* * *

The annual summer journey from Stornoway to Hull was always easier than the return journey. On the outbound trip Mammy and I would kiss Daddy goodbye on the quayside and board the Caledonian MacBrayne steamer, *Loch Seaforth,* at around 8:00pm, although it didn't set sail until much later in the evening by which time Mammy and I were usually asleep. We always had a two-bunk cabin and slept for most of the eight hours it took the vessel to get to Mallaig. Sometimes we were woken up a bit earlier when the boat docked at Kyle of Lochalsh two hours before it arrived in Mallaig if it was a particularly noisy docking. In the morning Mammy would take me down to the dining room on one of the lower decks for breakfast, but I could never eat anything. The combination of feeling seasick due to the movement of the boat, the smell of greasy food in the dining room and the fumes and vibration from the engines made me nauseous. I was never actually sick, but it was a close thing. When we disembarked at Mallaig at around 8:00am we went straight to the train station and caught the train for the relatively short ride to Fort William, where we changed trains and boarded the one for Glasgow Central. When we finally reached Glasgow, we normally stayed for an hour or so, had some food and waited for the train to York.

I remember Mammy telling me once that on a similar journey when I was a toddler she had gone to the 'ladies' and handed my reins to Daddy who was reading a newspaper he had just bought from Menzies. When she came back, I was not there so she and Daddy looked round in a panic and saw me just about to toddle out of one of Glasgow Central Station's exits. They shouted and Daddy ran after me and obviously I did not come to any harm. Daddy must have had some earache about that, but I know that he would have beaten himself up anyway without any input from Mammy.

We travelled in steam trains in musty-smelling compartments that held six passengers on two sets of three seats facing each other and luggage was stored in large nets on a metal frame above the seats. The compartments had sliding doors that opened onto a corridor running the full length of the carriage, past toilets at either end. If you stood in the corridor when the train went round a bend, you could see the long trail of steam flowing from the engine at the front. I found those journeys long and boring as a child, but I would give my eye teeth to take that journey though the beautiful Scottish countryside in a steam train now.

Uncle Ken and Auntie Doris always met us at York Station and drove us to Grandma and Grandad's house. I usually fell asleep in the back of the car and had to be woken up when we finally arrived there a full 24 hours after leaving Stornoway to a rapturous welcome from Grandma and Grandad. The school holidays ran from the end of June to late August, so I usually celebrated my birthday in Hull without Daddy. I loved when he finally arrived and gave me a big hug.

The homeward journey with both my parents worked slightly differently. Uncle Ken drove us to York where we waited in the station café and bar for the sleeper train to Inverness to arrive. We sat at the bar which served alcoholic and non-alcoholic drinks on red bar stools that, to my delight, could swivel round and round. I usually had lemonade, Daddy had a beer, and Mammy ordered her favourite drink gin and lime. Eventually the sleeper train arrived and when we boarded it, a steward led us to our reserved cabins. I always enjoyed lying in the top bunk in the fast-moving train listening to the rhythm of the metal wheels on the track and from time to time hearing the distinctive warning whistle. Mammy slept in the lower bunk and Daddy was in the cabin next door. In the morning the steward knocked on both our doors 30 minutes before the train arrived at Inverness and we dressed as easily as we could in the cramped cabin, disembarked and ate breakfast at the station café in Inverness station before boarding the train to Mallaig. I can still remember hearing the hiss of steam, the sound of the brakes locking, smelling the fumes and feeling the heat coming off the train from its hot coal furnace as we stood on the platform watching the Mallaig train slowly come to a halt beside us.

The journey onwards from Mallaig was the part I always dreaded. We spent eight hours on the *Loch Seaforth* again but this time during the day. The Minch is a stretch of water separating the Outer Hebrides from the Inner Hebrides and the Scottish mainland. It is very open and despite being summer, the swells were always unforgiving as the *Loch Seaforth* ploughed stoically through the strait. I tried to sleep, read a comic or play but nothing worked; my seasickness was a truly miserable experience.

Eventually my torment ended, and we would all go out on deck in the early evening as the boat came round Arnish Point with its distinctive but small white lighthouse and entered the bay of Stornoway Harbour where you had a panoramic view of Stornoway town. The spire of Martins Memorial Church and the steeple of the Free Church located on Kenneth Street stood out against the skyline. As we slowly approached the outer harbour, we would watch the small buildings including the Caledonian Hotel (The Cally) and cranes on the quay in the distance becoming bigger and bigger until we docked beside them. Ten to fifteen minutes later, after it had been securely attached, we trotted down the gangway, pleased to be on dry land and home. Sometimes, if we arrived on a warm evening, Auntie Agnes would be waiting on the quayside and wave to us as we came down the gangplank.

Chapter 4

Infant and primary school, Stornoway
1959–1966

I attended the Nicolson Institute which was the only school in the town. Our education was divided into three stages; two years in the infant school, five years in the primary school and then six years in the secondary school if you stayed for the full educational journey. Our school uniforms were navy, and our ties had navy and yellow stripes, incidentally the same colours as Hull University which I attended much later. The Nicolson's motto was 'Sequamur', a shortened version of the Latin "nos sequemur" meaning 'we will follow'.

I started school in August 1959 and remember holding hands with my best friend and neighbour, Isobel, as we skipped happily up Kennedy Terrace in our new school uniforms; we were very excited to finally be going to school. Isobel was slightly shorter than me, had thick straight fair hair that came down to her shoulders but was often held back from her face by a soft hair band, blue eyes and an infectious smile. Mammy and Isobel's mammy, who I called Auntie Rhoda, walked behind us.

Unfortunately, my happiness faded when we were led into the infant school hall where the rather scary and unwelcoming headmistress, with hair drawn back into a tight bun (whose name I can't remember), told us that we would be directed into one of two classes – Miss Macleod's or Mrs Mackenzie's. To my dismay, I was allocated to Miss MacLeod's class and Isobel was allocated to Mrs Mackenzie's class. I was distraught for most of the morning because I didn't know any of the other children in my class. Miss MacLeod was a small, unsmiling, very thin, middle-aged woman with glasses and grey hair parted at the side and held down by a hair slide. She always wore a pale blue plastic-looking zipped overall with a flared skirt. This was probably to keep chalk dust off her clothes as there was a lot of chalking on blackboards in those days. I didn't take in anything she said that first morning as I was mourning the loss of Isobel. Miss Macleod took the register, and the names meant nothing to me apart from one that made me think of a cushion. I later found out that it was Catherine McCuish of the tidy hair. Halfway through the morning, big grey crates were carried into the classroom by a man we were told was the Janitor, and we were all given a small bottle of milk with a paper straw. While I was blubbering into my milk, a different grey-haired lady crouched down beside me. She said her name was Mrs Smith and she had a kind face and asked about me, Mammy and Daddy. Through my tears I also told her about Isobel, and she said that I would be able to see Isobel at playtime. I started to feel a bit better then.

The infant school was a small brown stone building at the junction of Francis Street and Matheson Road, a five-minute walk from Daddy's office and he came to collect me at the end of the morning and took me home to have dinner with Mammy. Walking home at dinnertime with Daddy became a pattern that continued for many years, even when I was older. At lunchtime I would walk up

Matheson Road from the school and would look down Scotland Street which intersected on the left and often saw him walking towards me with his slightly hunched posture. I would wait for him to reach me and then we walked home with my arm looped into his. A less pleasant memory about dinner times was that after lunch Mammy would give me a tablespoon full of cod liver oil, which was gross, followed by a sweetener of five Smarties which helped but didn't fully take away the taste.

I gradually got to know the other children in my class and made new friends, so school became a much nicer experience.

In the second year of infants, we moved into the old clock school, presumably so the new intake could occupy the classrooms we vacated. The clock school was located on the same site and housed two classrooms in a distinctive brown brick building boasting a huge clock tower. It had two separate entrances leading from the playground. The entrance on the left led directly into Miss MacLeod's classroom and the entrance on the right led to Mrs Mackenzie's classroom on the left and to a corridor running to the back of the building. There was a door off the corridor with four glass panes and steps leading up to the clock tower itself. One of the panes was missing and if you put your head through the empty space, you felt a rush of cold air in the dark; we all thought it was creepy. We had a student teacher for part of year two; she was lovely and much more relaxed than the starchy Miss MacLeod.

At the start of the following school year, when I was seven, we trooped across the site to the primary school which was a plain-looking squared off two-story building with yellow rendering surprisingly called the

"Pink School". We were allocated into A and B streams based on the progress we had made in the infant school in terms of reading, writing and sums, and I was placed in the 'A' stream along with thirty-two classmates. Seven of us were left-handed and at that time we used fountain pens to write in our blue jotters with the Nicolson Institute badge on the front, so smudging was an occupational hazard. However, we were not forced to write with our right hand which had been Daddy's experience as a left-hander at school. He told me that they tied his left hand behind his back to ensure he didn't use it. That sounded very cruel to me as a child and from an adult perspective positively Dickensian. We slowly progressed through the education machine starting with lovely Miss Mackay in primary 3A who was very kind and supportive and helped us settle into the school and to

Primary 5A Class photo.
(Isobel is first from the left on the front row and I am standing up sixth from the left in the third row).

our new subjects. Both primary 4A with Miss McGregor, who was much younger than the rest of our teachers, and primary 5A with Mrs Kennedy, who was a widow and always dressed in black, were relatively uneventful.

However primary 6A came as a bit of a shock when we encountered strap-happy Miss Maclean, nicknamed 'Boring' and she was. The Lochgelly tawse or 'The Strap' as we called it, was used in Scottish schools up until 1998 as a way of maintaining discipline. It was a thick leather whip with one end split into two tails and it was designed to sting. Boring took the instrument very seriously and wielded it for the slightest infringement. The number of swings with the strap increased incrementally with each offence and some boys in the class went as high as six during that year. I experienced the strap once after the person sitting behind me said something and I turned around. I had to go up to the front of the class, place one hand over the other, palms up and she swung the strap down onto my hands. It really hurt and I could feel tears start to well up in my eyes as much with embarrassment as the pain, but I closed my eyes briefly and they subsided. Luckily, our wooden desks had metal legs and when I returned to my seat, I grasped one of the legs with both hands and the cold of the metal helped to reduce the stinging.

Primary 7A was a much more interesting year with Mr MacArthur, who was very tall and thin and bore the nickname 'Lofty'. His son, Ian Macarthur, who we called Carthy was in my class, but Lofty didn't give him any special treatment. Lofty had sallow skin and oiled back jet-black hair and always wore tweed suits. He sat on a tall chair with long legs like a bar stool and used to unnerve us by leaning back so that two of the legs left the floor. I think we could all envisage the possibility that one day he would tip the chair too far back and disaster would ensue. He was an inspirational teacher because he had seen a lot of life. The female teachers we had up until then were mostly spinsters and had lived very closeted lives on the island. Lofty brought an energy and worldly dimension to our education and stimulated our curiosity.

In year seven the academic pressure really intensified. We had completed an IQ test in primary 6A, but we didn't know the results. In primary 7A we had to take another IQ test and complete the 'qualifying examination' to determine our stream and class in the Nicolson Secondary School. England had a similar set of tests known as the eleven-plus.

The Nicolson Institute had an excellent reputation in Scotland for the number of students it sent to university. There was a kind of snobbishness on the island about the heights that individuals achieved in their chosen career and pupils knew a university degree was the key to giving you more choice and chances of success. In those days the country had only the traditional red brick universities and none of the modern universities we have today that were formerly polytechnics, meaning there were significantly fewer graduates competing for prestigious positions and that was a strong pull factor. If you did not go to university, the opportunities on the island were limited to working in the tweed mills, fishing, serving customers in Woolworths or the Co-op, which were the two biggest shops in the town, or doing the same thing in one of the many small retail shops who at best would have two or three staff. If you managed to get some O-levels, but no Highers, there was the possibility of the civil service, i.e. the Labour Exchange where Daddy worked or the Department of Health and Social Security or in one of the local banks, if there were any vacancies. The lack of opportunities on the island acted as a strong push factor.

After we had sat the qualifying examination, we relaxed and looked forward to the long summer holidays. We went to Hull for a shorter period that year and I spent time at the tennis and bowling club on Bayhead with Isobel and my other closest school friends, Fiona Kennedy, Jane Longbotham, Frances Grant and Lizzie Gillies.

It was 1966 and a memorable summer for football. Daddy and I watched the final between England and Germany together on our television on Saturday 30th July. We were both disappointed that the Scottish football team had not qualified but Daddy was happy to support a British team against Germany. I, on the other hand, decided to support Germany. Maybe I was just being perverse, but I claimed the reason was because I had a German pen pal. I had met Joachim Rolfe (Akki) who was the nephew of Grandma Trowell's neighbour, Irene, one summer when I was seven and he was nine and we were both in Hull at the same time. We spent a lot of time together and after he went home to Neustadt am Rubenberge and I returned to Stornoway we wrote to each other regularly. I had no knowledge of the German language but luckily Akki spoke and wrote English fluently. This long-distance friendship continued for a further eight years, but we never met again.

* * *

As the summer holidays came to an end it was time to prepare for going to the secondary school. Mammy took me shopping to buy replacement school uniform items, gym shoes, a new satchel, notebooks, pencil case, etc. It was an exciting time but also an anxious one. I was sure that I would not have failed the 'qualifying' but had I done well enough to get into the top stream, Class 1A?

Chapter 5

Bread and circuses or food and entertainment

During weekdays I spent a lot of time with my friends doing 'safe' things. Because my parents were older when they adopted me and had gone through the traumas of several miscarriages and a neo-natal death, they could be a bit overprotective at times. Many of my friends had roller skates but I was not permitted to have any in case I hurt myself, and I was not allowed a bike of any sort until I was 12 years of age. That meant that when some of my school friends went off on bike rides to the castle grounds or the beach, I couldn't go with them. Most of my close friends had siblings so they always had at least another non-adult around to spend time with at home. My neighbour, Isobel, had two sisters and a younger brother; Frances Grant had an older sister; Jane Longbotham had two older brothers; Lizzie Gillies had a younger sister and brother; Fiona Kennedy had an older sister and brother; and Jane Stevens had two brothers, one older and one younger than her. I didn't know anyone else who was an only child, and I often desperately wished that I had a sister or brother to be silly with in our rather serious house. I felt particularly lonely on Sundays and although I went to Sunday school, none of my best friends' families went to Martins Memorial church.

I remember reading that in Roman times, emperors distracted the citizens of Rome by ensuring that they had food and entertainment, usually in the form of the gladiatorial arena. There was not much to do on Sundays in Stornoway, so meals and television became the main highlights of the day. I didn't consider church or Sunday school to be highlights, they were just things I was expected to endure.

Daddy always finished preparing our Sunday dinner when Mammy and I returned from church and Sunday school. The meal was either small pieces of braised steak with carrots and roast potatoes, or mutton scraped off the bone accompanied by boiled potatoes and garden peas. These meals alternated each week, and we ate what was left over for Monday's dinner. The steak was okay for Monday because it had been reheated, but I thought the cold mutton with congealed fat was disgusting. I liked to go with Daddy to Charley Barley's butcher shop on Saturday mornings to collect the meat that he would start to prepare on Saturday afternoon. Charley's real name was Charles MacLeod but as there were many Charles MacLeods on the island it was a good way of distinguishing him from all the others. Charley had black hair, a small black moustache and wore a white coat with a blue and white striped apron over it and he and Daddy would have banter while Charley cut the meat from the carcases hanging on large hooks on a rail behind him. He would trim off the section of meat then put it on scales on the countertop, wrap it in greaseproof paper and put it into a thick brown paper bag. The counter in front of Charley where he weighed the meat was clean but there were bits of meat and blood in the sawdust on the floor. Surprisingly the shop did not smell bad, and

I assume that was because the meat was fresh. All I remember is the smell of the sawdust and an odour I can only describe as copper-like, maybe it was from the blood.

As a family we ate a lot of cod and ling, and it seems looking back now that we had dead fish on the draining board in our kitchen several times a week. I hated seeing their milky eyes, gaping mouths and the fishy smell that hung downstairs in the house for ages. Daddy regularly walked around the inner harbour where the small black fishing boats with their SY prefixes were moored, and he always came back with at least one fish. He knew all the fishermen because he dealt with them at the Labour Exchange when they returned home from their long fishing trips, and they always pressed fish on him. Occasionally we would eat a flat fish called a flounder. During my first year at school, I couldn't understand why we were given a day's holiday because of a fish. It was Founders' Day!

Of all the savoury food I ate as a child, nothing tasted as good as fresh salmon. Every now and again in the evening, usually after dark, there would be a distinctive knock at the back door and Daddy would wait a few minutes before he opened the door and brought in a newspaper parcel containing a salmon from a friend. I still didn't like seeing the dead fish's face, but I knew that the literally 'poached' salmon would taste delicious.

Standard puddings included fruit pies with custard. To be fair to Mammy, she made decent apple, gooseberry, and rhubarb pies and Daddy grew his own gooseberries and rhubarb in a little vegetable patch at the bottom of the garden. Sometimes we had tinned peaches, pears, or strawberries with evaporated milk.

One summer in Hull there was a bumper crop of strawberries and everyone we visited gave us fresh strawberries and cream. They were hard and tasted so different from the lovely soft sweet, tinned strawberries that I refused to eat them. Mammy told me later that she was very embarrassed by my behaviour.

Meals were generally eaten in our cramped blue and yellow painted kitchenette sitting on stools around a modestly sized fablon-covered table. We only used the big dining table with pull-out leaves in the living room when we had visitors because we could not seat more than three people around the kitchen table.

Sometimes on Sundays in winter, we had tea on a small two-foot square fold down table in front of the coal fire, usually sliced banana, or apple on toast followed by a Caramel Wafer or Blue Riband biscuit. The table had a glass top sitting over a tapestry and two hinges underneath so it could be folded down to stand flat against the wall. Auntie Agnes had a similar table, and I am fairly sure that the tapestries were made by Grandma Morison.

* * *

We got our first television when I was five and for some time, we were the only family at our end of the street to have one. I had watched television at both my aunties' houses in Hull but to have one in our living room was wonderful. Some of the first programmes I remember watching in the evening were *Bronco, Wagon Train, Laramie,* and *The Lone Ranger.* I loved westerns and dressing up and often sat engrossed on the floor in front of the set wearing my cowgirl outfit comprised of a black skirt, a fringed yellow and black waistcoat, hat, neckerchief, and plastic holster containing a light alloy gun. As I got a bit older, I was allowed to put caps in the gun to make it 'bang' when I pressed the trigger.

During holidays from infant school, I sometimes viewed *Watch with Mother* shows at two o'clock and watched *Andy Pandy, The Wooden Tops*, the *Flowerpot Men* and *Rag, Tag and Bobtail* puppets wobbling through a story, their strings clearly visible.

We were only able to watch BBC because television came to Stornoway through cable not from a transmitter to domestic aerials. Maciver and Dart, the main electrical shop, had cleverly enabled this to happen.

When important events took place, our living room would be full of friends and neighbours watching the television along with us. I remember that happening for Princes Margaret's wedding, President Kennedy's funeral and for the Cassius Clay versus Sonny Liston Heavyweight Title of the World fight. The fight in which the 22-year-old Cassius Clay (later to become Muhammad Ali) astounded the world by defeating Liston through a technical knockout in the seventh round by 'dancing like a butterfly and stinging like a bee'. I was ten years old and watched the fight with Daddy and Isobel's Daddy, Uncle Billy. I felt sorry for Sonny Liston and thought that Cassius Clay was very smug and big-headed.

Hugh Strachan, who was quite a bit older than me (maybe by five or six years) lived across the street three doors down from Jane Stevens and he came over late on Thursday afternoons for several weeks to watch a programme teaching art. I sat there quietly while he watched and wrote or drew in his notebook. When the series ended, he gave Mammy an oil painting he had created of a red flower in a flowerpot sitting on a windowsill, as a thank you gift. Mammy put the painting on the wall above the bookcase and it stayed there until we moved. I wondered if he ever became an artist and later googled 'Hugh Strachan artist'. I found a reference to the grave of an artist called Hugh Strachan, but he was born in 1912, so it was clearly not him.

* * *

One evening after tea, Daddy and I were sitting on the settee watching the news as we did most nights unless I was at Brownies. A very serious newscaster was talking about Cuba and Khrushchev and something about a missile crisis. I was eight at the time and had heard the name Khrushchev and seen footage of him in Russia on the news before, a small man with a bald head always looking very stern. I watched in alarm as the newscaster suggested that the crisis could lead to another world war. I went into the kitchen and out the back door and my dog, Timmy, named after the dog in the *Famous Five* books by Enid Blyton, followed me. There was a slope in our back garden with three steps and I sat on the top step, very worried about what I had just heard, cuddling Timmy. I remembered seeing a Sunday afternoon film about World War II with people screaming and running to underground shelters as bombs dropped. I looked round the garden and wondered if Daddy could dig some of it up and build a bomb shelter underneath so that Timmy, me, Daddy and Mammy would be safe when the war started. When I said my prayers that night, I asked God to stop the war. Then I looked under the bed seven times as

I always did and climbed into bed, but I couldn't sleep straightaway, I was too frightened. I don't know why I had to look under the bed seven times every night, I don't know if it was because I was an only child, had fears about the bogeyman, or something to do with an obsessive nature but I remember that compulsion continued for a few years.

***

One Saturday the following year I should have gone with Mammy to a 'Sale of Work' in Martin's Memorial Church Hall, but I had a slight temperature, so I spent the afternoon lying on the settee with a pillow and blanket and watched television. Daddy and I had just watched the football results with the names of the teams and the scores appearing as if by magic from the teleprinter accompanied by deep and monotonous man's voice saying something like, "St Johnstone 3, Alloa Athletic 2," and repeating the same process for all the matches played in the Scottish League that afternoon. The next programme to come on was the first episode of *Doctor Who*. I was fascinated by the storyline and didn't notice the wobbly sets and poor acting until much later. I couldn't wait for the next episode. I thought William Hartnell's character was very rude and when the Daleks first appeared in the fourth episode they scared me, but I was hooked, and this was the start of a life-long interest in time travel, space travel and all sci-fi. I love the creativity, escapism, and the feeling of 'if only' that time travel inspires in me and the fascinating notion that if a character travels back and changes something in the past, it could change history and consequently the present.

Mammy brought home a turquoise and yellow knitted tea cosy that we used for years afterwards, an iced cake and homemade tablet. She told me that if I ate all my tea, I could have some of the tablet which tastes like a very sweet crunchy fudge. I felt sad that she had missed *Doctor Who* and couldn't wait to tell her all about it.

Chapter 6

Secondary school
Stornoway 1966

I have always enjoyed the adrenalin kick of exams and have usually had good results. Thankfully the 'qualifying' was no exception. I discovered that I had done well in the tests and was allotted to the highest academic stream, Class 1A in the secondary school, which meant that in addition to the basic syllabus I also learned two languages. I had the choice of French and Gaelic or French and Latin. My family did not speak Gaelic, and I viewed it as a language that would soon become as dead as Latin, but how wrong I was. Having understood later in life how the defeat at the Battle of Culloden in 1746 led to the decimation of the Highland culture, clans, and the Gaelic language, I am now happy to see its revival. I chose Latin and enjoyed it despite having to memorise all the declensions and conjugations (Amo, Amas, Amat, etc.). The passages and poems we had to translate from authors like Catullus, Virgil, Cicero and Ovid, who had all died around 2000 years earlier, helped me understand and appreciate the impact the Roman Empire had on the development of civilisation in Europe and I marvelled at the sheer strength and power of Imperial Rome. I loved watching films like *Spartacus, Quo Vadis* and *Cleopatra* because although they were Hollywood's interpretation, they brought the detailed descriptions lying in the dead language vibrantly to life. Later, when work commitments took me to countries in Europe like Italy, France and Spain, my memory of Latin roots helped me with some local signage and basic vocabulary.

In both the A and B classes the basic syllabus for the first two years comprised English, History, Geography, Biology, Chemistry, Physics, Maths, Arithmetic, French and either Latin or Gaelic. Pupils who had passed the qualifying but done less well, were assigned to the F class where they had the same general syllabus but only one language, French or Gaelic. Primary school pupils from Stornoway and villages close by who failed the qualifying joined the non-academic streams and studied general subjects alongside more practical subjects like technical drawing for boys and home economics for girls. Pupils in the non-academic streams left school at the end of the fourth year.

The country villages across the island had their own infant and primary schools and those who passed the qualifying joined the 'townies' at the Nicolson Institute secondary school. So, in addition to new subjects to study there were new friendships to be made.

I started looking forward to my teenage years and what was to come, including the prospect of university somewhere on the distant horizon after sixth year. Class 1A was the first step.

Chapter 7

My search begins
Edinburgh, November 2008

In 2008 I was working for a Norwegian-owned paint and coatings company as HR manager for UK & Ireland and in November of that year, the decorative sales manager and I had arranged to meet members of the Scottish sales team in Edinburgh to address some concerns about the deco division's performance. I had decided to go there by train rather than drive so I could work during the three-hour journey.

I left Grimsby at 7:00am and arrived at the car park in the Frenchgate shopping centre adjacent to Doncaster station just before 8:00am and the car park was busy. The top two levels were reserved for rail passengers, and I liked to park on the covered fifth level, but that day I only found a free space on the open air sixth floor. I walked through the deserted shopping centre to get to the station; all the shops still had their shutters down apart from Greggs and there were only a few people walking around. As I stood on the descending escalator, I could see that the station ahead was much busier than usual which explained the car park. I made my way to platform 1 and sat in the chilly waiting room there until just before 8:30am when I went onto the platform and saw the train from King's

Cross approaching in the distance. After it stopped, I joined the bustle of people attempting to board the 8:30am East Coast train to Edinburgh. Finally, I found my allocated seat, unpacked my laptop, and went through the familiar challenge of trying to connect to the train's wi-fi system.

As a child, the long train journeys to Hull had seemed like a form of torture but as an adult, I loved travelling on trains and particularly this journey which called at York, Darlington, Durham, Newcastle and Berwick upon Tweed on the way to Edinburgh. The scenery was lovely, particularly on a sunny day and once we passed Newcastle; the train hugged the coast, and I could see the North Sea glimmering beyond the grassy fields for many miles. I had taken this route many times for both professional and personal reasons and it was always a pleasure.

Once the girls were grown, Glenn and I liked to celebrate our wedding anniversary on the 1st December each year by going away for a weekend near that date. Our two favourite places were Edinburgh and Stratford-upon-Avon, and we pushed the boat out by staying at the Balmoral Hotel in Edinburgh and the Shakespeare Hotel in Stratford.

The train arrived at Waverley station on time. As I walked along the platform, I could smell the strong diesel fuel coming off the stationary trains; the long, covered station trapped the fumes and if you had blindfolded me and placed that smell in front of me, I would have immediately said, "Waverley station," it was so familiar to me.

I arrived an hour before the meeting and as I climbed up the long flight of stairs beside the majestic

Balmoral Hotel with its distinctive clock tower that can be seen from almost anywhere in Edinburgh, I debated whether I should turn left or right on Princes Street. Although it was early November, the sun was shining, and there was no sign of the habitual Scottish rain so at least I wouldn't have to negotiate my way through the busy street carrying an umbrella. I decided to turn right and headed for the St James shopping centre to have some lunch in the Thistle Hotel and browse in John Lewis if I had time. I crossed Princes Street easily as sections of the road were closed to traffic due to the tram installation marathon which seemed to have been going on for decades. As I walked along, I could faintly hear the strains of the bagpipes being played by the piper on Waverley Bridge. The tune was familiar, but I could not place it immediately. I stood still for a moment to listen more carefully, and then I realised that the tune was 'Mairi's Wedding'. I remembered singing that song in our music lessons at primary school and the lyrics came back to me.

'Step we gaily on we go, heel for heel and toe for toe, arm in arm and on we go, all for Mairi's wedding."

Although I had lived in England a long time, there was something about the sound of the pipes and the words of songs that I grew up with like 'Mairi's Wedding', 'The Skye Boat Song' and 'Scots Wha Hae' that seemed to bring out my innate Scottishness.

The pavements were full of people, women and young girls with carrier bags bearing high street names like Jenners, Debenhams, M&S, etc., alongside empty handed smartly suited men and women. I assumed they were businesspeople in their lunch hour. I looked down at my grey trouser suit and realised that I also fitted into that genre. On my way to the centre I walked past the Neoclassical General Register House, built between 1859 and 1863, on my left and the mounted bronze statue of the Duke of Wellington on my right. As I walked along, an idea that had lain dormant since 1989 suddenly started to stir. A follow-up meeting in Edinburgh had already been arranged for the following week so, in the words of Baldrick from the *Black Adder* television series, a 'cunning plan' started to form in my mind.

* * *

My journey up to Edinburgh the following week followed a similar pattern only Doncaster station was not as busy, and I was able to park on the fifth level. In between emails, food, coffee, and people-watching as the train sped past fields, unused stations, and myriads of back gardens, some tidy, some not, I allowed myself to reflect on the personal dimension to this business trip. When I was 15, I gained some information about the circumstances surrounding my birth. Mum told me that my birth name had been Carol Ann Blyth, and they had decided to keep my two Christian names after the adoption because they liked them. She knew that my birth mother's name was Helen Blyth, and the family had emigrated to Australia from Glasgow in the early '50s. Helen had been in her late teens when she became pregnant with me and although the father wanted to marry her, the family thought she was too young and decided to return to Glasgow where I was born and subsequently adopted.

After I discovered this, I fantasised about meeting my birth mother, but daily life takes over; getting married and having two daughters in quick succession followed by the need to bring in some income to supplement Glenn's salary meant that for many years it was pushed to the back of mind. In 1989, I was watching TV one evening when a documentary came on about two birth sisters who had been reunited. Although the long-term outcome of the reunion was not positive as the sister who had been adopted proved to be very needy and too much for the other sister to handle, the programme itself was very emotional and triggered a strong need in me to start the search for my birth mother. In early October I wrote to New Register House in Edinburgh asking what I needed to do to obtain a copy of my original birth certificate. They wrote back within a few days saying the cost would be £8 and I would have to produce, *'documentary evidence of your identity in the name of Carol Ann Morison. A baptismal certificate, school certificate, medical card, insurance policy, driving licence or other document would suffice. An extract of abbreviated certificate from the Adopted Children's Register is not acceptable as evidence of your identity'*.

I was disheartened and concerned because all I had with my adopted name on were my abbreviated birth certificate and my marriage certificate. My O-level certificates had been lost over the years and everything else was in my married name.

The desire to access my birth certificate stayed with me and the following year when Glenn and I decided to go to Edinburgh for the Fringe Festival in August, I decided that I would take my abbreviated birth certificate and my marriage certificate with me and go to New Register House to speak to someone there in person and explain the situation. I didn't share my plan with Glenn.

We normally drove up to Edinburgh via the M62 and A1. For some reason that year we went a different route, and we were following the A68 when we passed through Tow Law. At a certain point you have to make a sharp right-hand turn onto another road to continue the route North, so Glenn indicated right and waited for a gap in the oncoming traffic. Suddenly there was a bang and a severe jolt, and we realised that a car had crashed into the back of our white MG Maestro. It was clearly a case of driving without due care and attention but predictably the policeman who helped us dismissed the idea when Glenn mentioned it, maybe because the driver was known to the policeman. To cut a long story short, several hours later we were heading back to Grimsby in a large AA van with our severely dented and undriveable car securely shackled to an angled trailer behind us. I concluded that fate did not want me to be reunited with my birth mother, so I had dropped the idea of searching until it resurfaced when I was in Edinburgh the previous week.

My reverie was interrupted by an announcement over the speaker from the guard telling us that we would shortly be arriving at Edinburgh Waverley. My stomach started to do flip flops, and I was suddenly nervous about what I may find out.

When the train stopped, I retraced the steps I had taken the week before until I was standing in front of General Register House. My thumping heartbeat was echoing in my ears as I climbed the steps to New Register House which housed all the birth, marriage and death records for Scotland. I told the receptionist that I had made an appointment to view my birth records, and she showed me into a small room with dark panelled walls and a large old wooden desk. She asked me to take a seat in front of the desk and told me someone would come to deal with me shortly. The room felt cold or maybe it was me. The few minutes wait was agonising between the adrenalin high and the two-edged sword of eager anticipation and worry about what I may learn. Three or four minutes later, a middle-aged lady with brown hair came in, introduced herself as Margaret Ross and sat behind the desk.

What followed next is patchy. I remember her asking me a lot of questions and checking the identity documents I had brought with me. She asked me about my adoptive parents, and I informed her that they had both died. She was obviously used to doing this and was very gentle and supportive, but she did ask me several times if I was sure I wanted to see the birth entry. I was adamant that I did. She asked me to wait for a few minutes to allow her to make the necessary arrangements. Ten minutes or so later, she came back and asked me to follow her. We went into another room, and I saw a very large leatherbound book lying open on a table. We sat on two chairs in front of the table, and she showed me the handwritten entry of my birth in the register. My hands were shaking, and my mouth was very dry.

Just as Mum had told me thirty-nine years earlier, I had been born Carol Ann Blyth and my birth mother's name was Helen McGettrick Blyth. I was born at 12:15am on the 20th of July 1954 at Homeland, 1014 Great Western Road, Glasgow. Helen's occupation was listed an Ordnance factory worker and her home address as 545 Scotland Street, Glasgow. That seemed like a coincidence as Daddy's family home was on Scotland Street in Stornoway. The spaces for the father's name, occupation and address were empty. When I saw the time of my birth written in the register, I gasped. I knew that the time of birth was only recorded for multiple births. "Was I a twin?" I asked Margaret Ross, but that possibility crashed and burned very quickly when she told me that in Scotland the time of birth is always recorded unlike England where it is only done for multiple births.

As she wrote down the details for me, I wondered how on earth I would be able to find Helen after 54 years. Margaret had obviously anticipated what I would be thinking and explained that there was an organisation in Edinburgh called Birthlink that attempted to reunite families separated by adoption. She gave me a Birthlink booklet and a form that I could complete and send to them. I was in no doubt that I was going to contact Birthlink.

After I left New Register House, I just had time to snatch a bite to eat before the deco sales manager picked me up in his car and drove us both to meet up with the sales team in a meeting room in the Ocean Terminal shopping mall to review the revised sales targets and action plans they had prepared following our meeting the previous week. Through the window I could see the royal yacht, *Britannia*, moored up, now a popular tourist attraction rather than a vessel transporting members of the royal family to distant parts of the Commonwealth.

Returning home that evening I explained to Glenn what I was going to do, and he was not very happy about it. I knew that he was worried that I would get hurt or be disappointed, but I was sad that he did not share my enthusiasm about the information I had discovered and the possibility that Birthlink could help me find my birth family.

***

I had completed and posted the Birthlink registration form the day after returning from Edinburgh. Glenn and I had been to Stratford for our anniversary weekend and on Tuesday 1st December 2008, our actual anniversary, I received an email from Kate McDougall at Birthlink which said:

Dear Carol Ann

Thank you for sending your completed Birthlink registration together with your documents. We have now entered your details, and this has resulted in a match with a registration made by your birthmother Helen. Unfortunately, some sixteen years have passed since Helen registered in 1991.

Can you please give me a call on 0131 225 6441 so that we may discuss this latest development in more detail.

I was ecstatic. Helen had tried to find me. That was such good news. I rang the number and was put through to Kate. She told me, "We checked our records and found that your mother had written two letters to Family Care, which was Birthlink's former name. One was dated 12th August 1991, and the other is not dated but from the content looks as though it was two years later. She said she lived in Footscray in Australia."

"Australia?" I gasped. That was the last thing I expected.

"Yes, she explains in one of the letters that she lives permanently in Melbourne and her children and grandchildren live there too."

I wondered if she had come home to Glasgow to have me adopted and then gone straight back to Australia afterwards.

Kate continued, "In the other letter she said that she was coming to Glasgow for six months and she gave details of the 'care of' address she could be contacted at while she was here if there was any news about you."

"So, two addresses, that's good, right?" I was starting to feel stirrings of hope.

"Yes. Let me explain how we work and what will happen next. We always operate as an intermediary because we want to make sure that the relationship will be safe before we put you in contact with each other. We will try to trace your mother using these addresses. Once we have, we will ask you to write a letter to her, but you will send it here and we will post it on. We will ask her to do the same. If everything goes well, we will then divulge contact details to both parties."

I checked my emails every day hoping for good news. On the 4th of December 2008, I had just come back from work and was checking my emails when I saw there was one from Kate and I opened it eagerly, hoping that Helen had been traced.

Chapter 8

My watershed year
Stornoway, 1967

When you reflect on your life, some years stand out from all the others for either good or bad reasons, or sometimes because they turned out to be a watershed that changed the whole future direction of your life. For me, 1967 was such a year.

Music is an important and pleasurable part of my life. I don't play any instruments, so I get my enjoyment from listening or dancing to music. I am still amazed at the extent to which a particular piece of music or a specific song can bring back clear memories. I was on a personal development course once where I was asked to write down in eight minutes my answer to the question 'Where do I belong?'. My fellow course members described places, times and cultures but I, without hesitation, wrote a list of some of my favourite songs and music including 'Albatross' by Fleetwood Mac; 'Parisienne Walkways' by Gary Moore; 'Nights in White Satin' by the Moody Blues; 'Hotel California' by the Eagles; 'You're still the one' by Shania Twain; 'Fields of Gold' by Eva Cassidy; 'It's Not Dark Yet' by Calum Scott, and many, many more. When I hear the first few beats of a song or instrumental that I love it feels like I'm sinking slowly into a deep warm bath. I feel completely encompassed and experience a powerful sense of belonging.

My love of music had started before Daddy bought me my first record player around Easter 1967, but his gift helped to accelerate my passion for it; the case had a textured plastic finish in two tone grey and blue and I was so excited. He gave me some money and I went down to Maciver & Dart's shop in Cromwell Street; they sold televisions, radios, record players and most importantly, records. I bought my first four 45 vinyl singles that day. They were called 45s due to the RPM (revolutions per minute) speed they were played at, they had a diameter of seven inches, and I believe that they cost between seven and eight shillings at the time. I bought 'Silence is Golden' by the Tremeloes; 'The Boat that I Row' by Lulu; 'Please Release Me' by Engelbert Humperdinck and 'Don't Sleep in the Subway' by Petula Clark.

Daddy spoiled me and often gave me unexpected little gifts. There is one that I still have and cherish 60-plus years on. In February 1960, he went to Glasgow for an operation to have polyps removed from his nose, I was five years and seven months old at the time. When he came home, he handed me a tiny book with a tartan cover and told me it was about Bonnie Prince Charlie. I had heard of Bonnie Prince Charlie and knew the haunting Skye Boat song 'Speed Bonnie Boat' about the prince dressing as a woman and escaping to Skye in a boat with Flora MacDonald, but I was still not able to read well. Picking it up later when I was able to read, I saw that the tiny book, which measured three inches by two inches, was subtitled 'The Story of the 45' and the 100 pages in the tiny book covered the final Jacobite

Rebellion that started in 1745 and ended with their bloody slaughter at Culloden on the 16th of April 1746. In the front of the book is written in capital letters 'TO CAROL WITH LOVE FROM DADDY 22/2/60'. My daughter, Tina, carried it in her silk pouch on her wedding day representing something 'old'. Now it sits in a drawer in my dressing table next to my jewellery boxes and to me it is the most valuable thing in that drawer.

***

Apart from owning my very first record player, another highlight of 1967 was going on a school cruise in May when I was still in the first year of the Nicolson secondary school. It was a seven-day school cruise to Sweden, Poland, and Denmark on the educational cruise ship MV *Dunera* which we boarded at Invergordon. I can remember some elements of the trip very clearly, but not others. I recall having a top a bunk in the Jellicoe dormitory on E5 with my friends and waking up in the morning to Cat Stevens on the ship's speakers singing, "I'm going to get me a gun." I adored Cat Stevens and had a big poster of him on my bedroom wall. Whatever happened to that song? It seemed to evaporate into thin air long before he became Yusef Islam in 1978.

I was seasick for the first day and a half as we crossed the turbulent North Sea but then things improved. I loved the big dipper at the Liseborg amusement park in Stockholm which made you feel as though your stomach was moving uncontrollably around inside your body. I can't remember the exact number of times that Anne Soval, who I was paired with for that visit, went on the extreme ride but it was quite a few. We were both quite hoarse from screaming when we arrived back at the ship that evening. I also loved the Tivoli Gardens amusement park in Copenhagen apart from the fact that the white skirt I was wearing split down the whole seam at the back when I went down a particularly thrilling slide. I took the 'Dunera' badge off my jacket and pinned it across the seam to maintain some form of decency.

I remember Yum-Yum, the Filipino chef who laughed all the time and rubbed his very large tummy in a circular pattern saying, "Yum, Yum." The same songs came across the ship's radio every day booming out of the speakers on every deck and one that still reminds me of that cruise is 'Happy Together' by the Turtles. It was probably the most played song on the ship, and I bought that record as soon as I got back to Stornoway. One of the vaguest memories is the visit to Poland where we took a coach tour through the cities of Gdynia and Gdansk. I remember the tour guide pointing out the damage to the buildings caused by gunfire and mortars during the war and I was surprised that 22 years after the end of World War II, the buildings had not yet been repaired. I understand that we went to see a demonstration of traditional polish dancing, but I can't remember much about that. That memory was probably overshadowed by the excitement of the Liseborg and the Tivoli Gardens amusement parks. We went to see the little mermaid in Copenhagen harbour and although she was called the little mermaid, I was disappointed that she was so small.

By the time we sailed back into Stornoway harbour on the *Loch Seaforth*, I had run out of clean clothes and came down the gangplank in my school skirt, a thick woolly cream jumper and a Mexican hat I had bought at the Tivoli Gardens. Daddy laughed but I think Mammy was a bit embarrassed because all the other parents were there.

In May I thought that 1967 was going well and I still had the school holidays that would start at the end of June and the Stornoway Summer Carnival events to enjoy. I was also entranced by the winds of change outside of our Stornoway cocoon. The anti-Vietnam demonstrations, the hippie movement, and the sudden appearance of the flower children in America promoting 'love not war'. Scott Mackenzie's single 'San Francisco (be sure to wear some flowers in your hair)', released in May, was played frequently on the radio that year and the words, *"There's a whole generation with a new explanation"* seemed to epitomise these changes and the optimism of that time. I was intrigued by the new fashion styles accompanying this youthful rebellion; kaftans, bell bottoms, tent dresses in psychedelic colours, flowers painted on faces and long hair on both men and women. I was so looking forward to going to Hull to stay with my grandparents for four weeks and I was planning to buy some of the new fashionable clothes in C&As with my saved-up pocket money. Then the runes were cast, and everything changed.

* * *

Mammy had passed her driving test two years earlier and my parents had a bought a white Fiat 600 which was bigger than the Fiat 500s that were produced at the time and are still popular today. Daddy started learning to drive in late Spring 1967 and a friend of his who lived on Leverhulme Drive was teaching him. One evening around the start of the school holidays, they came back early from the lesson and Daddy looked ill, he was grey and struggling to stand. I was sent next door to Auntie Rhoda's so I can't remember how they got him to hospital because we didn't have a phone to call an ambulance but that was where he ended up. Maybe Mammy drove him?

Details of the next few days are vague. I remember being told that Daddy would have to go by air ambulance to the Western General Hospital in Glasgow and Mammy was going with him. I was sent to stay with Auntie Agnes and Uncle Donald for a few days which unfortunately included a Sunday, and I recall having an argument with Auntie Agnes because I wanted to watch the film *Cool Hand Luke* starring Paul Newman on the TV on Sunday night. She resisted but Uncle Donald persuaded her to let me watch it and the tension in the air rapidly disappeared.

Daddy and Mammy came back after four or five days, and he was transferred to the Lewis hospital on Goathill Road which was five minutes' walk from our house. Mammy explained that Daddy had had an aneurysm in his brain which meant that a blood vessel had ruptured and was leaking. It had happened in an inaccessible part of the brain so although the doctors in Glasgow were not able to operate, they hoped that the ruptured blood vessel would seal itself and that meant Daddy would have to stay in Stornoway Hospital under observation for a week or two. I went up to visit him most days and he seemed to be gradually getting better and stronger.

I was looking forward to the Stornoway Tattoo, which was going to be held on Friday 21st July, the day after my birthday. One of my new friends from the secondary school, Alice MacLean who lived in Point, was coming to stay and we were going to the tattoo together. Even better, we were going to ride on the firemen's float in the Stornoway Carnival Parade on Saturday. The invitation came courtesy of Isobel's dad, Uncle Billy, who was a part-time fireman. His main occupation was as a joiner, and he had lost the top third of both the index and middle fingers of his left hand presumably through joinery. However, that did not stop him playing the accordion very competently in a ceilidh band that provided music at local dances. Isobel and her sister, Catherine, would be on the float as well.

The Stornoway Summer Carnival had started several years earlier to raise funds to build a swimming pool for the town. The island did not have swimming pool and the currents around the island were treacherous. The older son of the owner of the Caledonian Hotel had drowned a few years earlier and sadly I think that was one of the main catalysts.

My 13th birthday on Thursday 20th July was a muted affair due to Daddy being in hospital and we went to visit him in the evening. When we got onto the ward there was a curtained stand around his bed and a nurse told us that he had had a relapse. He was lying in bed not looking as well as he had the day before when he had been sitting in a chair wearing his red and wine striped pyjamas and wine silk dressing gown.

He wished me happy birthday, gave me a card and then he gave me a big hug and said a strange thing: "Look after your mammy."

"Of course, I will," I said.

We had to leave before the end of the visiting hour because he was tired and wanted to sleep.

The following day, Alice arrived, and we went downtown together. I had received postal orders from Grandma and Grandad Trowell, Auntie Joyce, and Auntie Doris. Auntie Agnes had given me money and Daddy had put money in my card. I wanted to save most of it to spend in Hull, but I also wanted to buy some records, so we went to Maciver & Dart. The shop always got records at least two weeks after they were released on the mainland but that was okay. Sometimes the records in Maciver & Dart were brand new but sometimes they had little plastic centres which mean that they had been played in jukeboxes before coming to the shop and these were usually a bit cheaper. That day I bought Scott Mackenzie's San Francisco' single and when I rummaged through the old jukebox records, I found 'Massachusetts' by the Bee Gees, so I bought that too.

We browsed around Woolworths and then went to the 'Ren-Den', that was what my friends and I called the Rendezvous Café on Cromwell Street which was the cool place for Nicolson pupils to go. We bought ice-cream sliders there, put money in the jukebox and listened to the records we had selected while we ate them. There were two cafes in Stornoway owned by different Italian families, the Capaldis and the Cabrellis. The Rendezvous was owned by the Capaldis, and I preferred it to the Lido owned by the Cabrellis. I consider myself lucky that I grew up with easy access to fresh, delicious, and genuine Italian ice-cream.

Alice and I went home for tea and then we got dressed up to go to the tattoo at Lews Castle which was part of the Stornoway Carnival entertainment programme. I put on my new dark blue bell-bottomed trousers that had been chosen from a catalogue along with a blue tee-shirt. As the tattoo started at 7:00pm and clashed with visiting hours Mammy was okay with me not going to see Daddy that evening. We walked down to Bayhead and crossed over the bridge to the castle grounds. The castle was an impressive building nestling in the only forest remaining on the island. Between 1844 and 1851 it was built as a country house for Sir James Matheson who had bought the whole island a few years earlier. In 1923, Lord Leverhulme bought the estate and gifted the castle to the people of Stornoway.

There was a sweeping patch of grassland directly in front of the castle and that is where the tattoo was held. We met up with school friends and bought some soft drinks and later some food from the stalls, then we went to watch the entertainment programme including the Stornoway Pipe Band, marching displays by the Territorial Army and the Boys' Brigade, dancing, music and singing all performed by locals. Donnie B was the commentator for all the Stornoway Carnival events and a few years later he became an announcer on Grampian TV. The evening was crowned by a wonderful firework display which lit up the sky above the castle just before 11:00pm. Alice and I had really enjoyed the evening and the freedom of going there by ourselves. When we got home, we were very tired and went straight to bed, looking forward to being part of the Carnival Parade the following day.

* * *

In the morning Mammy knocked on my bedroom door and asked me to go to her bedroom. I was worried by the tone of her voice. What had I done wrong this time?

When I went into the bedroom, I was surprised to see Uncle Donald there. He asked me to sit down on the bed which I did, and he knelt in front of me, took my hand and told me that Daddy had died during the night. I didn't take it in right away. He said that he would take Alice home and the minister would come and visit us later. I remember asking naively if I could still go on the carnival float and being told firmly by Mammy that it was out of the question.

Mammy then proceeded to close all the curtains in the house as was the local custom and I knew they would remain closed until after the funeral.

It was only later that morning when I looked in the birthday card written by Daddy sitting next to the wooden clock that he wound every Saturday night that I started to realise I would never see him again and then the tears came and didn't stop.

Chapter 9

Helen's search
Grimsby, December 2008

The email Kate had sent from Birthlink seemed to take an age to open. My eager anticipation that she had traced Helen crashed and burned when the second sentence of the email jumped out at me. It said that Helen had died ten years earlier.

I read the rest of Kate's email through a wall of tears. I had been so surprised and happy to hear that Helen had been searching for me that I had started to expect that I would get to know her. Now I knew this would be impossible. I had left it too late!

However, the email contained some interesting information.

Dear Carol Ann

I have now heard from the lady living at the c/o address who is in fact Helen's younger sister Violet. Sadly, Helen died some ten years ago. However, I have a contact address for one of your half-brothers in Australia whose name is William, and I will be happy to write to him on your behalf to progress contact with the family. There is also another half-brother Thomas and a half-sister Linda. All three are married with grown up family.

Violet also shared a little more background with me. Please be in touch and let me know if / how you would like me to proceed.

Kind Regards
Kate McDougall

I called Kate the following day and she told me that Violet had been born in 1944, so she was only ten at the time of my birth. However, she remembered that my father's name was Johnny Rankin because of all the rows, crying and upset at the time but Helen had never really told her much about the circumstances of my adoption. Violet had told Kate that their mother was a very strong person who ruled the roost, and no one stood up to her. The family had emigrated to Australia to live but when she found that Helen was pregnant, she brought the whole family back to Glasgow to get her away from 'him'.

Helen took her family to Australia in the 1970s to have a better life but came back to Glasgow regularly and stayed with Violet while she searched for me. Violet had confirmed that the others in Australia knew nothing about me. She told Kate that she had sent all her family photos to Australia, but she would see if she could find any from when they were younger. If she did, she would send them to Birthlink.

I told Kate that I would like to write to Violet and I asked if she would send me copies of Helen's letters. She said she would and advised me to start preparing a letter to Violet, telling her all about me, but she explained that she would not send it on to her until January as Christmas was an emotional time for families. I started drafting the letter immediately, hoping that at some point I would be writing 'Dear William' instead of 'Dear Violet'.

* * *

A few days later, I received a letter from Kate containing Helen's original letters handwritten, on thin lined paper torn out of an exercise book.

12th August

Dear Sir or Madam   (An official stamp below this said 13 August 1991)

Could you please help me as I've been trying for so long to trace my daughter whom I was made to give up for adoption 37 years ago. I've finally been given this address by the O.P.C.S. in England as they said as my daughter was born in Scotland this is the address to contact for further assistance. My daughter's birth name was Carol Ann Blyth born in "Homeland" unmarried Mother Home run by the salvation Army on 20-7-54 Gt Western Road, Glasgow. She was given to adoptive parents on 14-11-54 and as far as I could find out they were flying back to Germany same day so the man must have been in HM Services. I could never find out anymore but have been in touch with groups to no avail. This is my last hope as I don't want my daughter going through life thinking she was an unwanted child. I have so much to tell her. She does not have to think of me as a mother but as a friend I would love to know she was treated well and that she was happy. I can put her in touch with her natural father who would like to hear from her as well though we both married different people. Hoping you can help.

Yours sincerely
Helen Hudson

34 Faskin Road
Crookston
Glasgow

There was a postscript written on a second page using the same paper and blue ink.

I leave here on 28th August to return to Australia as I've been 6 months trying to find her, but I have to return back as my family is there, otherwise I wouldn't be going back. I get back here every six years & I try every way I can to try to find her, but I won't approach her myself I'd ask the Welfare to contact her first & find out whether she wanted to make contact or not. I'll go by her wishes. My address in Australia after 28 August.

Helen Hudson (Mrs)
8 William Street
Footscray 3011
Melbourne, Victoria, Australia

The second letter was written in black ink and had no date.

Dear Mr Lock

I had written a couple of years ago asking for help in trying to find out something about my baby daughter whom I was made to get adopted as my mother said I had to adopt her. I didn't want to, but I wasn't strong enough to stand up to my mother. You wrote to me in Australia and said if there was any news, you'd let me know, I'm now home in Glasgow and as you never got in touch you probably couldn't trace her. I've tried so many times through the years. Even if she didn't want to contact me, I just want to know she's OK and at least some good came out of the adoption. I'll never forget her as long as I live. I love her so much and always will. I'm married and have 3 sons and one daughter. I love my kids so much & I've been lucky I know as my kids are so good to me & I'm still with the man I married. I live permanently in Melbourne Australia & all my kids and grandkids are there. I'm here for a few months I thought I should get in touch with you. All I have is your address and name I forgot the file no. I'll give you the details again.

Child's name was "Carol Ann Blyth".

Born "Homelands Salvation Army unmarried mothers' home. Great Western Rd, Glasgow

B/date 20-7-54, was adopted from "Homelands" 14.11.54. I found out she was taken to Germany the same day, so I think the adopted father was in the services. I used to write to the Welfare asking for them to get me a baby photo, but no-one ever bothered to reply. She had a small round birthmark on the back of her right leg and the bluest eyes ever seen in a child. My single name was Helen Blyth, 545 Scotland Street, Kinning Park, Glasgow. I hope you have some information to give me and I appreciate your trying to help me.

Yours sincerely
Helen Hudson

P.S. I'll be here for some time as I have a job so
please write to me
c/o Envis
28-13 Glenorchy Drive
Glasgow

I smiled when I saw the reference to the birthmark on my right leg, it was still there and had grown bigger as I had. The letters made me feel very sad for her. She had tried for so long and so hard to find me and just wanted to know that I had been cared for and was happy, but she had died with her questions unanswered. Self-recriminations do not achieve anything but if the trip to Edinburgh in 1989 had gone differently or if I had persisted afterwards rather than dropping the search, Family Care would have been able to start a process of bringing us together when she registered with them in 1991.

I realised that she must have been relatively young when she died ten years earlier. In 1998 I was 44 years old and assuming that Helen was around 18 when I was born that would have made her only 62. It made me think about Daddy who had also died relatively young, he was five years younger than Helen when he was taken.

Chapter 10

Lost
Stornoway, 1967–1970

The days leading up to the funeral seemed unreal, Auntie Doris, Auntie Joyce, Uncle Stanley and Lesley came up to Stornoway as quickly as they could. Sadly, Uncle Ken couldn't get away due to his work. The curtains in our house were still closed, and the darkness and perpetual hushed tones just added to the illusory atmosphere. Neighbours would creep in and whisper with their gifts of home-made cakes and other items of food as if rapid movements or loud voices would break something. It was the summer holidays, but I wasn't allowed out to play, Mammy said that would be disrespectful with Daddy still at the undertakers and what would the neighbours think? I tried not to think of him being at Macrae's Undertakers on Keith Street. Daddy was only 57 when he died, he had not even made the three score never mind the three score and ten years promised in the Bible. Although parents always look old to us as we are growing up, looking at pictures of him taken during his last year through the eyes of a mature adult, I thought he looked much older than 57.

On the evening before the funeral, the undertakers brought Daddy's coffin to the house. Living room furniture was moved around and the coffin was placed in the corner of the room where the television usually stood. The coffin was sealed. Auntie Agnes, Uncle Donald, neighbours, and our minister, Colin MacLean, came to the house for a wake which I knew would be a depressing affair of prayers and spoken psalms. Thankfully, I was sent next door to Isobel's house.

Even although it was a sunny day in July and I was wearing a lightweight pale blue wool coat to the funeral service, I felt very cold and shivery as we walked into Martins Memorial church. The whole thing felt unreal, and I had a strange feeling of detachment as I saw the undertakers bring in the coffin, almost like it was not happening to me. Mammy had on a black dress and a black hat and looked very pale beneath her face powder. She was not wearing lipstick. She was dry-eyed during the service, but Auntie Agnes' eyes were wet. I cannot remember much about the funeral service apart from trying to sing the 23rd psalm 'The Lord is my shepherd' unsuccessfully, my mouth like the rest of me felt numb. I am sure nice things must have been said about Daddy, but I have no recollection. After the service, Mammy, my three aunties and I stood on Francis Street in front of the County Hotel opposite the church watching the hearse heading off very slowly to the cemetery. Uncle Donald walked in front of the hearse and Uncle Stanley walked at the back of it. Walking behind Uncle Stanley were all the men in Stornoway who had known Daddy, friends, neighbours, colleagues, and Labour Exchange clients. Wearing black or dark suits and black hats, with heads bowed they set off to follow the coffin solemnly on its one-and-a-half-mile journey to Sandwick Cemetery that would be Daddy's final resting place. Women and children were not allowed to go to the grave until the coffin had been lowered, the grave filled in and the flowers placed on top of the mound. We walked back to Auntie Agnes's house for coffee and waited for the uncles to return.

About two hours later, Uncle Donald and Uncle Stanley came back to Woodside from the cemetery. I had passed the cemetery many times on the way to the Braighe, a beach that sits between Stornoway and the small peninsula that is called Point, but I had never gone into it before, and I was a bit apprehensive. The sun continued to shine that afternoon as Mammy, Auntie Agnes, Auntie Doris and I rode to see the grave in Uncle Donald's two-tone grey Austin Cambridge. No one spoke during what seemed like a long, painful journey, although it probably took less than 15 minutes. I had seen church graveyards on films on the television and they always seemed overgrown and untidy. Sandwick Road Cemetery was not overgrown, but the assorted sizes, colours and aspect of the different gravestones and monuments gave a chaotic impression as if the layout of the plots had been decided on a whim. Daddy's name was not on the family headstone, there was just a mound of earth covered in flowers. While we were paying our respects to him and crying silently, I wished and wished that he would come up, put his arms round me and tell me that there had been a terrible mistake, it wasn't him in the grave at all.

I stared at Grandma Morison's name etched on the headstone; it was heartbreaking to think that only eight years earlier Daddy had been standing at her newly dug grave in the same way we were now standing at his.

* * *

Mammy and I went to Hull a few days after the funeral. Uncle Stanley, Auntie Joyce, Auntie Doris, and Lesley had left two days after the funeral as they had to get back to work. We flew to Glasgow and got the train from there to York where Uncle Ken met us.

Our time in Hull that summer was vastly different compared to previous years when I loved visiting all our relatives and spending days exploring and enjoying the features, pace, and noise of the big city. Everyone was kind but the long hugs, shaking heads and sympathetic eyes made me feel worse and reinforced the feeling that our lives had changed and would never be the same again. I remember spending a lot of time in Grandma's front room by myself reading or listening to her Bush transistor radio and I discovered a pirate radio station spinning records somewhere out in the North Sea. The station had a number, something like Radio 270 and like the other pirate ships played the most recent record releases unlike the BBC Light Programme which tried to please all age groups and satisfied none. That summer there were some great songs that still take me to that front room. Andy Fairweather Low's strangled rendition of 'Gin House Blues' as Amen Corner's vocalist and Procul Harum's 'A Whiter Shade of Pale'. Three years later, Uncle Ken took me to see Procul Harum playing that number live during a concert at Bridlington Spa along with the more sombre but equally enigmatic 'Homburg'. The year 1967 was when pirate radios became illegal, and the North Sea radio station closed while I was still in Hull that summer. The last record played was 'Land of Hope and Glory' and the irony was not lost on me. When it was time to go back home, I was very torn. I wanted to go back to see my friends, but I dreaded the thought of being back in our house without Daddy. It had been strange enough when he was in hospital but at least I had been able to visit him.

* * *

When I went back to school in August, I felt different from everyone else, and I knew that I had changed. Religion was the cornerstone of life and beliefs in Stornoway, and I had embraced it as a child. I had prayed to God to stop a world war after the Cuban Missile Crisis and there had been no war, but I had started to have some serious doubts about his 'goodness' when I watched the Aberfan disaster on television in 1966. Surely when Jesus said 'Suffer the little children to come to me' he didn't mean 116 of them suffering and dying along with 28 adults when the colliery slag heap engulfed the little village school. Now he had let Daddy die. I became increasingly cynical about God so the Bible reading we did at the start of every school day became a meaningless exercise to me and I wondered how the teachers and my classmates didn't question it – were they delusional or brainwashed?

* * *

All my classmates had two parents and most of them had siblings as well and they probably did not know what to say to me. I felt a deep gulf develop between myself and friends I had known since I started school, so, I decided to make some new ones. The Nicolson secondary was the senior school for children who had attended the infant and primary schools in Stornoway, but it also took pupils from the village schools on Lewis and Harris who passed the qualifying. Most of them lived some distance away and there were separate boys' and girls' hostels in the town to cater for them. They arrived by bus on Monday morning, stayed in the hostel during the week and went home on Friday after school. I got friendly with Maggie, Candy and Annie who all came from Lochs and that was fine because we had not had any kind of relationship up until then so there was nothing to get worse, only better. I was still pally with Isobel, but she took different classes from me, so I didn't see much of her during the school week.

I still went home at dinner time but found as I approached the junction of Matheson Road and Scotland Street, I couldn't stop myself looking for Daddy. After weeks of torturing myself, knowing that he would not be there but unable to stop myself looking, I changed my route home. Instead of following Matheson Road and Robertson Road to Leverhulme Drive where there was a cut through to Kennedy Terrace. I went along Springfield Road, up Smith Avenue and across Goathill Crescent to Leverhulme Drive.

***

I had always been a bookworm starting at the age of six with Enid Blyton's *Secret Seven* books then moving on to her *Famous Five* series. I know that I read 19 of the 21 *Famous Five* books but could not tell you which two I missed. From there my interest in mystery became a bit more sophisticated and I moved onto Agatha Christie and followed both nosy Miss Marple with her unique insight into human behaviour and moustachioed

Hercule Poirot with his 'little grey cells' with great interest.

When I was 13, I started to feed the interest in sci-fi piqued initially by *Dr Who* and reinforced by films like *The Time Machine* and *Invasion of the Body Snatchers*. The Stornoway library had a science fiction section, all the books in there had yellow plastic covers with 'SF' written in red ink on the spine, and I devoured them hungrily. One book helped cement my thoughts about religion; I cannot remember the title, but it was about a spaceship that had been travelling through space for several generations and the closed, unnatural environment had led to some birth mutations along the way. The aspect of the story that struck a note with me was the fact that all the passengers kept referring to 'The Ship' and revered it like a deity through worship and fear. Over the generations they had forgotten what the spaceship was, and its name had taken on a whole different meaning, they had even made-up fantastical stories about 'The Ship'.

Could we have distorted stories about a young man who spoke common sense to gatherings in the Middle East 2000 years earlier and elevated him to be the son of an omnipresent and omniscient supreme being? We knew from science that the planet had evolved over millions of years, not six days, and we knew about the human need to make sense of things by creating gods. The Ancient Egyptians, Romans and Greeks all had their different gods, and they believed, wrote about, and worshipped them too.

***

No surprises that my marks in the tests at the end of year two, as I was coming up to my 14th birthday, were unremarkable; it had been a horrid year. My favourite subject in year two was English taught by Charlotte Murray, who was funny and a bit eccentric, and that was the one subject where I achieved high marks. The following year, a new head of English, Mr Whiteford, arrived and he took over the top group that I was in. He was an inspirational teacher and his enthusiasm for the written word flowed out of him. English as a subject in Scottish schools was a combination of English language and English literature, unlike English schools where they were treated as two distinct and separate subjects. Mr Whiteford treated us as if we were students, not pupils, in contrast to Mr Horne who hit you over the head with his book if your Latin translations were not up to scratch. We obviously had to follow the standard English syllabus, but he encouraged us to expand our interests and read other books, plays and poetry. We read Shakespeare and Chaucer, and I enjoyed both; in contrast we read Harold Pinter's dark and atmospheric plays, and Dylan Thomas' free verse poetry alongside the more classic iambic pentameter variety. He encouraged us to stretch the boundaries of our creative writing, and I realised I had found that sweet spot between something I really enjoyed and something I was quite good at in that English class.

It was probably a reaction to Daddy's death but early in year two I had started thinking that I would like to be a doctor, but I was very average in maths, biology, chemistry and physics. My pure enjoyment of English and my essay marks in year two and year three made me totally rethink this and I decided that I would like to 'read English' at university, as they said on *University Challenge*.

* * *

Following Daddy's death, our household income reduced significantly so Mum had to get a job to supplement Daddy's pension and the state widow's pension which was derisory. So, she was out of the house for the full day, Monday to Friday, working in an office in Kenneth Mackenzie's Harris Tweed mill. I lost a lot of confidence during year two and put on weight because without realising what I was doing, I was comfort eating and would often buy chips followed by chocolate for lunch rather than go home to an empty house. Mum must have been comfort eating too because she bought lots of sweet things like cakes and chocolate which exacerbated the problem.

I spent a lot of time alone in my bedroom playing my singles and later my LPs. The first two LPs I bought were *Bookends* by Simon and Garfunkel and *Disraeli Gears* by Cream. They were extremely different, but I enjoyed both the melodic and lyrical harmony of the former, and the stirring vocals, screaming guitars and maniacal drumming of the latter.

When you have been touched by death, the world becomes a much darker place, and you become acutely aware of your own mortality. I started to regard the self-righteous churchgoers as cowards. Believing 'the Lord is my Shepherd' and in an afterlife in Heaven meant you didn't have to think about asking the question, what will happen when I die? Psalm 23 answered it for them:

'Yea through I walk through the valley of the shadow of death, I will fear no evil for thou art with me, thy rod and thy staff they comfort me'.

I felt as though I was in the valley of the shadow of death alone. Mum was suffering too, and although she was in the house after work and at weekends, she was not fully present. I knew she was taking some tablets, but at the age of 13 I didn't know much about antidepressants or their effects. I guess I was depressed too and in 1967 there was no bereavement counselling. The only potential source of support was the minister, and I no longer believed in what he offered, so I just had to get on with it.

I took solace in reading my books and playing my records in my bedroom and felt a connection to, and empathy with, some lines from Paul Simon's Song 'I am a Rock':

I have my books and my poetry to protect me.
I am shielded in my armor.
Hiding in my room, safe within my womb
I touch no one and no one touches me.
I am a rock.
I am an Island.
And a rock feels no pain.
And an island never cries.

A few months ago, I heard an announcer on Mellow Magic radio, refer to a particular song as time travel music. When I hear 'I am a Rock' and other music that I used to play in my bedroom, they transport me back to that sad time and place so vividly.

Chapter 11

Good news or bad news?
Grimsby, January 2009

In early January 2009, Kate called me to say that William would like to hear about me so if I could send introductory letters for both him and Violet to her, she would send them on. I was relieved. After finding that Helen had passed, I hadn't wanted to face another disappointment, so I worked on the draft I had already prepared for Violet and then customised it for William. Unfortunately, I did not keep copies of these letters, they sat in my old laptop and were lost forever when it gave up the ghost. I remember that I started off saying something like this was probably the hardest letter I had ever had to write because of not knowing the impact my news would have on them and their families. Then I went on to describe details about growing up, the main highlights of my life up to that point and enclosed some pictures of me and my family. I was on tenterhooks afterwards waiting to see what, if anything, would happen next.

On the 13th of January 2009, I received a letter from Kate in which she had enclosed two photographs from Violet and her contact details, she confirmed that Violet would like me to call her. Kate had added a handwritten P.S. saying that she had just received an email from William saying that a letter and photos were on their way. I didn't know what the letters would say but even if they politely told me never to contact them again, he was sending photos and at last I would be able to see what members of my birth family looked like.

I looked at the photos Kate had enclosed. One was of Helen and my half-sister, Linda, who looked to be in her mid-teens, they were both wearing long dresses and were standing in front of a band with drinks in their hands. Helen's hair was dark and tied back. There was a definite a family resemblance between Linda and me, particularly our colouring and face shape.

Helen and Linda on board ship.

The other photo was of two women sitting together and on the back Violet had written that Helen was the one with the grey curly hair. Unfortunately, somewhere along the way I lost the second photograph.

It was Saturday, Glenn was having a lie-in after a late shift the previous evening and I rushed up the stairs and sat on the bed. He looked at the photos through sleepy eyes and commented on the resemblance between Linda and me.

* * *

I decided to call Violet on Sunday evening. I counted my blessings that she had received the letter and replied because Kate told me that Violet no longer lived at the address in Helen's letter. However, Violet's surname was Envis which was quite unusual and the postal worker who was given the letter to deliver recognised the name and took it to her new address. Maybe fate, which had ensured that Helen and I would never meet, had started to take pity on me and was trying to redress the balance. I was a little apprehensive as I keyed in Violet's phone number. She had replied very quickly to Kate's letter and had sent the first photos I had ever seen of Helen, but I knew I was opening Pandora's box and there would be no return.

The phone was answered by a woman with a Scottish accent, speaking in a strong Glaswegian dialect. "Hullo"

"Hello, Violet it's Carol Ann."

"O ma goodness, Carol Ann, I wis sae happy to get yer letter I ken Helen wid have been tae but it's too late fir her, poor soul. She came back home tae Glasgae manys a time looking for ye but she niver got anywhere and she'd come back to the hoose in tears. I ken one day she was upset cos she said ye wid be 40 that day."

"I was really pleased to get her letters and know that she didn't want to have me adopted," I replied. It was one of the questions in the back of my mind over the years – why didn't my mother love me enough to keep me?

"You sound sae posh, Carol Ann"

"I'm not posh, I just have a very different accent."

"Aye ye dae and that's reet but ye were brung up in Stornoway huh?"

"Yes, my dad was from Stornoway but met my mother during the war. She was English."

"Are they still wi us?

"No, my dad died when I was 13 and my mother when I was 31. I had no brothers or sisters so you can imagine my surprise when I found out I have a half-sister and half-brothers in Australia."

"An aw the time Helen was looking fer ye, she thought they'd taken ye tae Germany."

"Please tell me about Helen, there's so much I want to know about her and her life."

"Helen lived for her family, and she worked very hard to gi'em a better life. Well, a better life than she had anyway; Ma was an old witch. She wis very strong an all she thought about was money and neither Da nor Helen could stand up tae her. When we started work, we had tae hand over all oor wages tae her so we niver had any money that's why Helen couldnae keep ye."

She told me she didn't remember much about Australia, apart from the fact that it was too hot, she was only nine when the family returned to Glasgow. I asked her about my natural father, but she had only a vague recollection of him.

"He wis called Johnny Rankin an Helen wisne allowed tae see him. Ma would make Helen take me wi her when she went oot so she couldnae spend time wi him. Ah ken one time when she an im went canoodling and Helen made me stand watch in case Ma came. I wis there for ages."

I didn't want her to feel that the telephone conversation was an interrogation, so I stopped asking questions for a while and listened as she told me about herself and her family. I learned she was a nurse working night shifts at a psychiatric hospital, that she had married Alex young, and they had two sons, Colin and Alexander. She loved karaoke and dancing and going on cruises, sometimes with Alex but often with friends. I asked if she and Helen had any other siblings.

"Aye, Tom's a braw lad and he lives in Glasgow wi Lynne and the other tae are in Australia as well. Bill's nae a nice person like Tom, an Caroline is over there tae. She was born in 1961 and I alus thought Ma called her Caroline tae get back at Helen because Carol Ann and Caroline dinae sound sae different. Ma treated Helen so bad but ma Da was better tae her but he couldnae stand up tae Ma."

I was starting to wonder about Helen and Violet's mother and asked for their names so I could try and search for information on them through New Register House. Violet's parents' names were William and Mary Ann but on an everyday basis they were called Wullie and Nancy. Apparently, the grandchildren were not allowed to call them Grandma and Grandad, Mary Ann

Helen, Violet and their sister-in-law Lynne
on one of Helen's visits to Glasgow.

had insisted that they were called Mammy Blyth and
Daddy Blyth. Violet confirmed my assumption that
Helen's middle name, McGettrick, was her mother's
birth name, a tradition in Scotland at that time.

"My parents liked Carol Ann, so they kept the
name Helen gave me. I often wondered where my name
came from, although I expect it was quite a common
name in the '50s."

"Helen's first baby wis called Ann."

I was stunned by her statement. The story Mum
had told me about Helen becoming pregnant young and
the family coming back to Glasgow despite the father
wanting to marry her was understandable, but Violet

was now saying that Helen had been pregnant before me, I started to wonder what kind of person Helen had been.

"How old is Ann?"

"Aboot a year older than ye and she's in a wheelchair."

"Do you see her, is she in Glasgow?"

"Nae, she's in Australia tae wi the rest of them. Helen took her family over to Melbourne in 1970s fer a fresh start, Glasgae was nae a happy place then. She went over wi Linda for a year tae work and get some money and left Rock, Linda, and Tommy back here with Sammy."

"Who's Rock?"

"William, the whole family call him Rock cos that's wit he is, Helen alus said that."

"Helen wrote letters to Family Care around 1990 and said that she had one daughter and three sons. You mentioned William and Tommy, was Sammy her third son?"

"Nae, Helen was married tae Sammy. Ah forgot wee Stevie he wis only aboot three when they left."

"Did Ann go over at the same time as Helen?"

"Nae she went over later. Ann wis born in Australia so it was easier for her to gae than Helen."

The knowledge that Helen had had a baby in Australia before me knocked me for six, so I started asking more general questions about Helen, where she had lived and what she had done, where she worked. I didn't take in too much of what she said next because I was still reeling from the Ann revelation.

I was sitting in our large wood panelled hall on the antique sofa with its beautiful carved back and arms that used to belong to Auntie Agnes. Glenn called from the kitchen, "Food's nearly ready."

Although I was desperate to find out more about my birth family, I needed time to think. When you know you're adopted, your mind seeks out possible scenarios. The positive ones included being a stolen baby princess who'll be found and restored to the palace one day, that was when I was young enough to believe in fairy stories. Later, the idea of a loving mother and father who lost everything but wanted the best for me and someday would come looking for me, appealed. As I got older, I wondered about young love cruelly torn apart like Romeo and Juliet, and the story my mum told me about Helen's circumstances fitted with that. But Violet's news about Ann opened a door in my mind with a dark recess behind it. Was the story my mother had been told a smoke screen? I rapidly closed the door and mentally locked it with a big key.

"Sorry, Violet, my tea is on the table, I need to go but I'll call you again soon, there is so much more I want to know."

I decided that I would wait to see what William's letter said about Helen and Ann. Depending on how I felt after that, Glenn and I could always take the four-hour train journey to Glasgow to find out some more information from Violet and combine the trip with a weekend in Edinburgh.

I had so many questions. I needed to know more about Ann and wanted to understand why Helen had made the momentous decision to take her family halfway around the world to start a new life in Australia in the 1970s.

Chapter 12

Fresh starts
Hull 1970–1971

In July 1970, Mum and I started a new life in Hull. I don't think that Mum was ever happy in Stornoway and that unhappiness became more intense after Daddy died. She was never a relaxed person but in hindsight I think she was a bit neurotic, always anxious and restless. I was a self-centred teenager so I didn't really appreciate what she was going through or how lonely she must have felt in the narrow-minded and religion-fixated fishbowl of Stornoway. She had been half of an entity called Kath and Rody for over 20 years and now she was just Kath. In addition, she had been a housewife and stay-at-home mum, now she had to work five days a week in an office.

I was 15 and in the fourth year studying for my O-levels when she told me about her idea for us to move to Hull. I don't know if she had been planning to go back to Hull ever since Daddy died or if it came to her gradually. When she told me, I was ecstatic about the prospect of living in a big city with everything going on. In my naivety I had no idea of the enormity of the decision and what a difficult transition it would be for a teenager with low social confidence because of what I saw in the mirror. I still had this uncontrollable hair and was slightly overweight, the result of too much chocolate comfort eating and not enough exercise. I started wearing black clothes because I thought the colour was slimming and over the years that became an ingrained preference of mine. The weight issue was magnified in my mind by the fact that most of my friends were very slim and pretty. I always went to the school socials at Christmas and at the end of the academic year but was always a wallflower and I was never asked to dance. This reinforced my lack of self-confidence.

I compensated for this by developing a kind of intellectual snobbery reading widely and outside the English curriculum. I devoured the works of James Joyce, Dylan Thomas, Leonard Cohen, Saul Bellow, DH Lawrence, Yeats, Ted Hughes and Emily Bronte. I also started to enjoy biographies on historical figures like William Joyce, known as the traitorous Lord Haw-Haw during the Second World War, Leon Trotsky, an architect of the Russian Revolution, Jean-Paul Marat of the French Revolution, Howard Carter, the archaeologist who discovered Tutankhamun's tomb, Archibald McIndoe and his plastic surgery guinea pig club during World War II, and became fascinated by the lives of Che Guevara, Fidel Castro and the Cuban Revolution.

I found a partner in crime, Nan Morrison, from Fidigarry. We were on the same wavelength and shared a passion for literature. Her father was the headmaster of the Fidigarry school and as the village was just under nine miles from Stornoway she did not need to stay in the girls' hostel. Nan was very serious, slim and slightly taller than me with short brown straight hair, brown eyes and a sprinkling of freckles. During the fourth year we were inseparable. I recall going to a film night in the school with her where we watched *The Caretaker* by Harold Pinter followed by a slapstick film involving Eric Sykes. We both laughed hysterically throughout the slapstick film unlike the rest of the audience. Discussing it later with Mr Whiteford, he believed it was because both Nan and I had really understood and absorbed the darkness in Pinter's play and our hysterical laughter had been an antidote.

* * *

Mum and I left Stornoway on Thursday 16th July 1970. A large removal van from Hull with 'Hardaker' written on the side arrived late morning and the removers started to load our furniture onto the container vehicle and packed other belongings we had already wrapped in newspaper into vintage wooden tea chests.

It was very strange looking around the empty living room with its pale patches on the wallpaper where pictures had hung and darker patches on the carpet square where furniture had stood. I had so many memories of being in that room with Daddy.

I went up to my bedroom for the last time and reflected on what had been my personal space since I was a toddler. I was not sure how quickly I would have a room of my own again that would depend how quickly Mum was able to find and buy a suitable house. In the meantime, Mum and I would share the double bed in Grandma's front bedroom. In my bedroom I could see the mark on the carpet where the folded Z bed's metal frame had stood. When I was small, I slept on that Z bed and there was a double bed in the room for family from Hull to sleep on if they came to

Stornoway, although that was infrequent because we went to Hull most summers. As I got older the Z bed was folded and stored in the corner of the room, and I progressed to sleeping in the double bed which was up against the wall. I always slept facing the wall with Teddy beside me. About the same time, I was allowed to get involved in the selection process for new wallpaper for my bedroom. Daddy brought home large wallpaper books from Charlie Morrison's hardware shop on Point Street where the smell of rope and turpentine hit you as soon as you went in the door. I chose a wallpaper with a pink and gold pattern and the skirting boards, window frames and the bedroom door were painted pink to match. As I looked around the bedroom, I could see all the tiny holes in the wallpaper from the drawing pins that had held my posters of Cat Stevens, Scott Mackenzie, David McCallum aka Illya Kuryakin and Che Guevara securely to the walls. Dr Kildare's poster had been relegated to the bin a few years earlier.

I looked out of the curtainless window to the view I had seen first thing every morning and last thing every evening for many years. The Stornoway slaughterhouse lay directly beyond the wall at the bottom of our garden, I often wondered why it was in the middle of a residential area surrounded on three sides as it was by houses on Kennedy Terrace, Westview Terrace and Jamieson Drive, but it was an old building, so it was probably there before the council houses surrounding it were constructed or even planned. There was a large rectangular open area in the middle, pens around the side for sheep and large metal hoops fitted to the wall bordering the back gardens of our houses on Kennedy Terrace where cows would be tethered by ropes.

Every Wednesday cattle trucks rolled up to the slaughterhouse and reluctant cows and skittish sheep were led out. If we were not at school, Isobel and I often sat on the wall and talked to the sad-eyed cows chained on the other side although we were both a bit afraid that they would break free of their ropes and come into our back gardens. Sheep were crammed into smaller pens close to the slaughterhouse building itself and there were some larger pens bordering Westview Terrace. In the late morning, crofters arrived, and we listened to the auctioneer's clipped and rapid-fire attempts to increase the price of each animal. Those not sold never returned home and during the late afternoon we would hear loud gunshots echoing from the corrugated metal slaughterhouse and see the workers coming in and out of the building wearing their long leather aprons and hosing down the tarmac's surface. The smells of animal and death dominated the air even when there were no animals there.

Another reminder of death was the Lewis war memorial sitting on top of the 300-foot-high 'Cnoc nan Uan' hill directly in line with my window. The 85-foot-high memorial is shaped like a Scottish baronial tower and was constructed from local gneiss stone and granite. The decision to construct a memorial was taken in 1920 to commemorate the 1,151 men from Lewis who lost their lives fighting in World War I and advertisements in *The Stornoway Gazette* urged local people to make donations as the cost was estimated to be more than £10,000. When the fund reached £5,000, an anonymous donor, who turned out to be Lord Leverhulme, added a further £5,000. The memorial was completed in 1925. Over the years because of its exposed nature, the building suffered water ingress from heavy rainfall and various attempts were made over time to repair it. In 2017, a major restoration took place costing an astounding £230,000 but some parts of the interior are still not accessible.

In my almost 16 years in Stornoway, I had never heard about the *Iolaire* and only found out about it from a BBC documentary made in 2019, 100 years after the disaster. Amongst the 1,151 Lewis men commemorated by the memorial were 200 Royal Navy reservists who tragically drowned on New Year's Day, 1919 within sight of Stornoway Harbour when HMY *Iolaire* transporting them home from France hit rocks called the Beasts of Holm and sank in a storm.

I said a last sad farewell to the room that had been my refuge for so long and walked down the carpetless staircase to the front door and out through the open porch where I had played houses with Jane Stevens and other friends.

Many decades later I wrote a poem involving my bedroom, the view and Stornoway on Sundays.

SY (Stornoway)

Clinging to her sunny dream, the girl slides out of bed into the monochrome room, a tear crawling out of her eye.
From her window she sees a memorial to the dead standing high on the hill, framed by the sullen sky.
She wonders who they were, young, older, single or wed?
Did they march with pride and glory; or fear that they may die?
Death shrouds her thoughts today; it won't get out of her head.

The slaughterhouse is silent, no cows will die today
It's Sunday on this chilly isle; sermons and ministers' rule.
Childish joy smothered, while the adults sing and pray
Swings padlocked, shops shut, only the churches are full.
While sinners cringe in their Sunday best, children long
to play.
Washing lines empty, TVs turned off, no one risking
ridicule
or public shame for defiling the Sabbath Day.

Replete with fish, peat and heather moors,
They decry the mainland and its' heathen lives
while some embrace hypocrisy behind closed doors.
The girl, longing for so much more, hopes the day arrives
when she can escape this place forevermore;
to laugh, kiss and dance in discos and other dives
and do things the brainwashed elders would abhor.

* * *

Mammy had sold her Fiat 600, so Uncle Donald took us down to Sandwick Road Cemetery in the afternoon to visit Daddy's grave and say goodbye to him. That was upsetting because I did not know if, or when, I would come back to Stornoway again.

We went back to Auntie Agnes' house where we had tea and waited until it was time for my aunt and uncle to take us to the Loch Seaforth around eight o'clock. We had said goodbye to Isobel and her family earlier and Auntie Rhoda said it would be strange not to hear me singing on the other side of the wall.

I had been a Brownie and a Guide and, after that, a Ranger Guide. We used to meet in the Scout Hall on

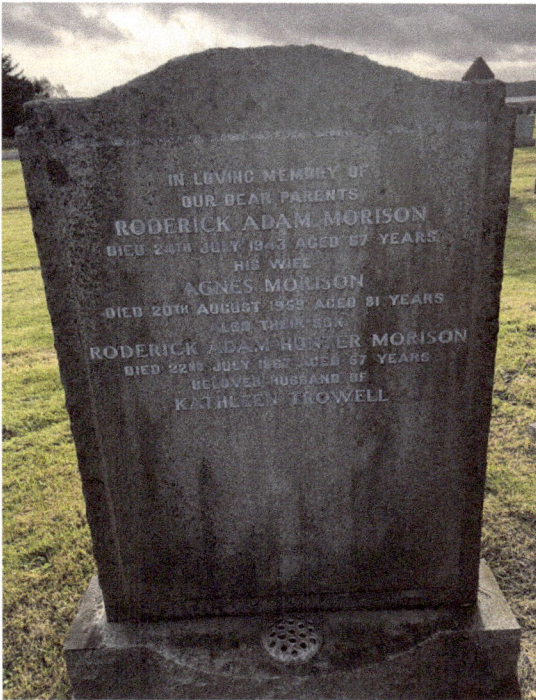

Daddy's Grave.

Keith Street every Tuesday even during the summer holidays; we were more of a social group than serious Ranger Guides. I had decided not to go the week we were leaving as I didn't want any fuss. That Tuesday evening, I was up in my room playing my records and packing my clothes when there was a knock at the front door. Two of my friends, Ishbel MacMillan and Frannie Grant, had come to persuade me to go to Rangers. So, I conceded and went with them. When I arrived, I was presented with the *Nashville Skyline* LP by Bob Dylan which I still have. I thought that would be the main farewell, but I was surprised and delighted to see some of my friends, Lizzie Gillies, Fiona Kennedy, Jane Longbotham, Ishbel MacMillan, and Frannie Grant, with their boyfriends on the quay beside the Loch Seaforth when we arrived there in Uncle Donald's car on Thursday evening. We all hugged and as I walked up the gangplank and waved to them, it dawned on me really for the first time that I was leaving everything and everyone that was familiar. It was a strange sensation, exciting but scary at the same time.

* * *

We arrived at Grandma Trowell's house on Friday 17th July 1970 in Uncle Ken's car. Grandad had died in April 1968, so she was now on her own and we were going to live with her until Mum found our new home. Uncle Ken loved music as much as I did and although he was in his 50s, he kept up to date with new releases and the pop and rock music scene. He told me that the Incredible String Band were performing at Hull City Hall on Sunday evening and that he would be taking me to see them as part of my birthday present from him and Auntie Doris. I would turn 16 on Monday 20th July. I was extremely excited because we had talked a lot about the Incredible String Band in the Ren Den in Stornoway, and I was familiar with their 'psychedelic-cum-traditional' folk music. He told me that his friend, Malcolm, had also got a ticket so we would all go together. I loved spending time with Uncle Ken, but I was not sure about this Malcolm because I had never met him.

That summer, Uncle Ken took me to a pop festival in Halifax and I remember us both sitting in huge black plastic bags on a hillside in the rain. I was not familiar with any of the bands, there was no major headline act, but the music was live and good, and the novelty of the experience was brilliant.

* * *

Malet Lambert School was on James Reckitt Avenue in East Hull just around the corner from Auntie Doris and Uncle Ken's house on Gillshill Road. The red brick building was Neo-Georgian, imposing and covered in ivy. My cousin, Lesley, had gone there, and it had been a co-ed grammar school with a good academic record. In 1968 it became a community comprehensive school as part of the Labour government's plans to phase out grammar schools and secondary moderns and replace them with comprehensive schools. Mum was looking to buy a property near to Auntie Doris so although she had not yet found a suitable house, it was logical that I attend the lower sixth form at Malet Lambert.

In the Nicolson, pupils would study five or six subjects to 'Higher' level. In England I knew that you would normally study three at A-level, so I had some choices to make. I was dreading my O-level results but was pleasantly surprised when they arrived. I had gained 'A' grades in English, History and Latin; a 'B' grade in Arithmetic (statistics) and 'C' grades in Maths, Physics, Chemistry and French. I was relieved that I had passed French because I had not been able to sit one of the two papers due to sickness. Uncle Ken presented me with a glossy book of Leonard Cohen's song lyrics as a reward for passing all my O-levels. After much consideration I decided to choose English, History and French for my A-level subjects.

My eager anticipation about going to the sixth form evaporated quickly on the first morning when we went into our lower sixth tutor group with Miss Robinson. She had curly ginger hair, glasses, no make-up, and a facial expression devoid of any hint of warmth or humour. She laid down the rules, insisted that we all wore full uniform every day and she called the boys by their surnames. Not at all what I was expecting after the freedom I had experienced at the Nicolson. I gradually got to know other girls in the tutor group and found out that some of them were a year older than me because they had repeated their O-level year. I made friends with Liz Naylor, Helen Klink, and Jean Rodgers.

I quickly started to hate subjects that I had previously loved like English and History. English literature was turgid and the first book we had to read was *Mary Barton* by Elizabeth Gaskell written in 1848. I never liked Dickens, and this was along a similar vein. I missed Mr Whiteford's energy and enthusiasm. History was similarly boring, focusing on the Ottoman Empire, an era I knew nothing about and frankly didn't want to. French was the weakest of my three subjects, but we started reading a novel called *Les Dieux ont Soif* (The Gods are Thirsty) by Anatole France which was set in Paris around the time of the French Revolution, a period I found fascinating. I struggled with the translation but enjoyed this so much more than English or History.

Unfortunately, I rapidly started to lose interest in school. I would go to Miss Robinson's tutor group where the register was taken but would often then sneak out of the school and cut across East Park to Summergangs Road, where Mum had finally bought a house and spend the day playing my records or reading a book. Dreams of university started to fade because I couldn't stand two more years of this. Eventually my poor attendance record was noticed, and I was invited to the headmaster's office. He was very patient with me and was concerned that the academic performance of someone with eight O-levels had taken a nose-dive at his school. He suggested that it may be better for me to try a different school where I could make a fresh start. He spoke to Mum, and they agreed that I should transfer to Newland High School, the school Mum had attended. I was not happy for a number of reasons; it was a girls' school, and I had always been in a mixed school, it was in West Hull so I would have to take two buses to get there, and I would have to start to make new friends again. Mum made it clear that I did not have a say in this decision.

It was December and an interview with Miss Nicolson, the headmistress of Newland High School, had been arranged. If all went well, I would start at the school at the beginning of the January term. The interview was arranged for an afternoon in December, a day or so before the end of term. At lunchtime that day, Liz, Jean, Helen and I went to the Pelican pub on James Reckitt Avenue, about 10 minutes' walk from Malet Lambert. We all looked 18 or older and with winter coats covering our school uniforms we had no problem being served. We each bought and drank two Cherry Bs. Cherry B was a popular sweet red alcoholic drink at the time that came in small bottles that filled one and a half wine glasses. It was about 14% proof and by the time my friends put me on the bus at a bus stop further down James Reckitt Avenue and waved goodbye, I was feeling distinctly tipsy. I had to change buses in town to get to the school so I hoped that by the time I got there

I would be sober. Looking back now, I wonder if I was deliberately trying to sabotage the interview or if it was just as simple as my schoolfriends having a leaving celebration with me.

***

As I walked through the gate to Newland High school, I could see that the building was a carbon copy of Malet Lambert. I hoped the rest of the experience would not be a carbon copy too.

I was shown into Miss Nicolson's office and sat down on a seat in front of her desk. She was a thin, unsmiling middle-aged woman with short grey hair and glasses. I was quite shocked because the first thing she said to me was, "Have you been drinking?" I shook my head vigorously and strongly denied it. I don't know if she believed me, but I started at the school in January 1971. I had been told that I could not do history because the class was already too large. I asked about Latin, but they were not teaching Latin. Some form of madness must have seized me because I opted for A-level economics instead. Why? I had not done the O-level and knew nothing about it. Also, I had missed the first term. I would have been better off staying at Malet Lambert trying to catch up.

I stumbled through to the Easter break, hating every minute of school and the two-bus journeys. When school reconvened after Easter, I had made my mind up, I was going to leave. I knew that Mum would be angry, so I decided to try to find a job first to try to mitigate her reaction. I went to the careers centre in Hull, told them I had left school and went through the rigmarole of registering for work. Then I went back to school and decided to wait patiently until I was notified if a job came up. The next day I was summoned to Miss Nicolson's office and went in there to find that the man I had spoken to at the career's office was also there. Talk about Big Brother! He said that I could not register for work if I was still at school, it had to be one or the other, so I told him and Miss Nicolson there and then that I wanted to leave school. Miss Nicolson contacted Mum and that evening we had an almighty row.

I find it quite ironic that Newland High School, the final scene of my teenage academic failure, is located next door to the Hull University campus where, in 1981, as a mature student, I achieved a BA Honours degree in Sociology and Social Anthropology, class 2:1. This was followed by a Post Graduate Diploma in Personnel Management in 1986 and a Master's degree in Business Administration (MBA) in 1991.

I stayed at home, going into the careers centre every few days to see if there was any work. It was a miserable time. Mum and I were hardly on speaking terms, I was bored and had no money to buy records or new books to alleviate the boredom. Because of my love of music, I thought it would be interesting to work in a record shop and while I was in town visiting the careers centre, I would go to Gough & Davy's Music Shop, hoping to see a 'staff wanted' postcard in the window, but none appeared. About two months later, I was notified about a records clerk position (sadly not the right kind of records) at Pouparts & Co, a fruit and vegetable wholesaler in Humber Street. I was given a six-week trial which I passed. The work was boring, recording delivery notes and invoices in ledgers. However, there were two other girls in the same office, Bernadette and Cathy, and they were fun to be around.

When I got my first weekly pay packet of £6.50, I was so excited that I went out at lunchtime and bought two new blouses and a skirt from Marks and Spencer to wear for work. I had not had any money for ages, so it felt great. When I arrived home that evening and showed them to Mum, she was cross that I did not give at least some of my first pay packet to her as board and lodge.

Although the relationship with Mum was quite strained, there was obviously some kind of family powwow going on about me because Uncle Ken told me that Gordon Ransome, who was a family friend and connected with the hospital in some way, had said that there was a vacancy for a trainee technician in the Biochemistry lab at Hull Royal Infirmary. Uncle Ken explained that it involved day release at the Technical College in Queens Gardens in the centre of Hull to gain the relevant qualifications. When he asked if I was interested, I said yes because I was. I had O-level chemistry, and I knew I needed some focus and prospects for the future now my university dream had died.

Gordon sent the paperwork, and I competed the application. Two weeks later I received a letter inviting me to an interview with the chief Biochemist, Jim Parks. I psyched myself up for the interview and it was not as difficult as I thought it would be. A week later I got a letter offering me the position of junior laboratory technician, with effect from 1st September 1971. I had not felt so happy or relieved for a very long time. Maybe this would be a proper fresh start after the debacle and disappointment of the two Hull schools. Maybe I could become a scientist like Dr Spencer Quist and Dr John Ridge in *Doomwatch* on TV. I and all my friends in

Stornoway had had desperate crushes on the hunky Tobias (Toby) Wren, played by Robert Powell, in the series and were distraught when he was killed in an explosion while trying to defuse a bomb at the end of the first series.

I had asked for a chemistry set for Christmas when I was ten. I got the set, but I was not allowed to use the small paraffin heat source designed to achieve the same effect as a Bunsen burner, so I was never able to create reactions. The only experiment I was able to do was to mix potassium permanganate crystals with cold water, shake and see the water turn purple in the test tube. Chemistry at school had been quite theoretical with a strong focus on chemical formulae, molecules, atoms, and the respective positive or negative charges of protons and electrons. I hoped that the Biochemistry lab would be more hands-on and exciting. Looking back, I think I liked the idea of being a scientist more than I liked science.

Chapter 13

Brothers and sisters
Grimsby, February 2009

The days passed and I had still not heard from William and the disappointment only added to that post-Christmas anti-climax in a wet and gloomy January. As the months morphed from January to February, I rang Kate, concerned that William had changed his mind about writing to me. Kate told me that she had received a letter and photos from William and that she had forwarded them to me at least two weeks earlier. I was gutted, of all the mail to go astray why did it have to be that correspondence? Fate was playing silly beggars with me again. Kate said that she had an email address for William so she would let him know that I had not received his letter and photos.

Just over two weeks later I got a bulky envelope with a Birthlink stamp on the front, and I was impatient to find out what was inside. There were photos and a letter. I glanced at the photos but did not know who-was-who, so read the letter to see if contained more information about the people in the photos. It was a copy of the original one that had gone missing.

13 January 2009

Dear Carol

I was very happy and pleased to hear from you. It is very, very, sad to write this letter as you said since my Ma has passed on. I know she would have been over the moon. I am glad to be able to share all about my Ma with you. I adored my Ma she was a wonderful, loving and very proud woman who lived for her family.

I know she never forgot you and I cannot even begin to imagine the pain she went through and carried with her throughout her life. I remember Ma telling us about you in the late 1980s, (which turned out not to be true, I think Billy was trying to reassure me) *so I am not surprised she tried to find you. I am glad she did let you know that.*

I truly do not know how to begin this letter. I was very taken aback when Violet rang me before Christmas to tell me about you.

I was born on 12th May 1956 in Scotland. My sister Linda was born on 27th December 1958 followed by Thomas (Tom) on 15th April 1960. Our brother Steven was born in early 1970s. I am terrible with dates, but I think his birthday was 23 August 1971.

My Ma would be thrilled to know you had a good life and have done so well.

We lived in Glasgow until the early 1970s when my Ma and Linda went to Australia and worked hard to save the airfares to bring the rest of the family over. I know they had it hard, but my Ma had real determination and wanted a better life for us all. In Glasgow we really struggled and sometimes lived in only a single end in the early years, so I truly understand why she brought us to

129

Australia. I did not come with them at first, I was about 17 and an apprentice bricklayer and stayed behind. My Ma became ill, and Grandad lent me the money to fly over and see her and I stayed. I met my future wife Barbara over here and we went back to Scotland in 1977. We got married over there and tried really hard to make it work but found it hard and came back to Australia when we were having our first child, William, who was born in 1978. I have three children, another son Ryan who is twenty-nine next month and a daughter Bonnie who is eighteen.

My son William is a plumber and married to a girl also called Carol. They have a foster son Matthew who is four years old, and they had their first baby last October, her name is Illaura Shai.

My son Ryan is married to a girl called Kate and they have three children, Liam who is nine years old, Blake, who is 3 years old and little Ava who is eighteen months' old. Ryan is a carpenter. I am a bricklayer, so I think trades run in the family. I work for myself. My wife Barbara is a Claims Manager for a car insurance company.

I am sorry if I am rambling a bit, but I have so much to tell you and I don't know where to begin. My Ma was a very hard-working woman who worked all her life. Ma worked mainly in factories and cleaning jobs that sort of thing. In Scotland she worked in a lemonade factory called Henry's who made the soft drinks for the co-ops. Ma also worked in a biscuit factory called Grey-Dunns and they made blue ribband biscuits and penguins.

Growing up I remember living in Scotland Street and I went to the local primary school. The factories my

Ma worked in were nearby. My Da worked in factories also, a place called Howdens off Scotland Street. Ma was a bit of a gypsy, and we were always moving even if it was only up to the next Close or the next street.

I went to Scotland Street Primary School, and I have read in recent years that it is now a heritage building for art students. We always seemed to live in the old tenements around Tradestone which was in an area called Kingston, they built the Kingston Bridge nearby. I went to high school but left at fifteen to take up a trade. In Australia Ma worked again in factories and cleaning jobs. The last place I remember was her cleaning at a deaf school.

Linda works in factories and cleaning jobs as well. She is married to Frank, and they have two children, Belinda who is thirty and Frank who is twenty-three. Belinda has two kids with her partner Ian, Aliya who is thirteen and Christopher who is six.

Tom is married to Sylvia and her family came from Ireland when she was little. They have two children Kurt who is twenty-two and he and his partner Sam have a little one named Seth. Amy his daughter is twenty-one. Tom has done well for himself over the years. He left school really young and worked in factories and then in a plumbing supply shop. He worked his way to an area manager position. Tom now works as a prison officer.

Steven has never married, and he has no children, he works as a forklift truck driver at the docks.

Ma shared some of the same interests as you. She loved reading murder and mystery; she loved music, and her favourites would have been Elvis, Tom Jones and Shirley Bassey. Her favourite foods were fish *suppers and square sausage. She made the best home-made soup and loved chocolate, had a real sweet tooth.*

I think working hard runs in the family. I have so much to tell you and hopefully we will be able to talk on the phone.

I have enclosed a few photos of the family taken at Christmas and at Linda' fiftieth birthday, I am going to see Linda and Tom this weekend and I will tell them about you and show them your letter. They are both currently away on holiday.

I will get copies of all the photos we have of Ma, and I will send them to you. We do not have many, she never liked having her photo taken but I do have a couple of when she was young. I also have a couple of photos of our grandparents, I am not sure if you know much about our grandparents, but I can tell you about them in the next letter.

I wish you and your family well and I hope to hear from you soon.

Best Wishes
William
(everyone calls me Billy)

I was overwhelmed by the warmth in the letter and studied the photos trying to find any kind of resemblance. I could see that Linda and I still had a familial resemblance. Billy had a moustache so not so easy to see if we were alike or not, although two years later when my son-in-law, Jack, met him, he saw a resemblance between Billy and myself.

I was intrigued about some of the things he mentioned in the letter. What was a 'single end'?, and I had never heard of 'square sausage' despite growing up in Lewis. A single end turned out to be a one-room apartment in a tenement block where the whole family lived, ate, and slept with separate bathroom facilities shared by all tenants. I could not imagine the challenges that must have posed for Helen, her husband and presumably three children at that time. Square sausage turned out to be minced meat, rusk and spices formed into a block and then sliced. Probably closer to a burger than a traditional sausage.

He had given me his home address, email and phone number and sent me an email a few days later saying that he would call me on Sunday. I noticed that there was no mention of Ann in the letter.

* * *

I was sitting at the old pine kitchen table on that significant Sunday, 1st March 2009, the one that opened a new chapter in my life. The pine table had been one of Glenn's numerous bargain buys. It initially sparked his interest as an advert in the *Grimsby Evening Telegraph* before being meticulously transported into his bargain notebook through precision cutting and Pritt-Sticking. The end result was Glenn's declaration as he came through the kitchen door one weekend after a fishing trip to Hornsea: "I've got something in the boat, and I need a hand with it."

Yes, he had picked up the second-hand pine table and chairs on his way home. They were unhappily perched on his 16-foot fishing boat attached to his Subaru Estate on the other side of the street. The pungent smell of raw fish attaches itself to anything in the immediate vicinity and I was acutely reminded of that fact as we carried the furniture into the house. The table and six chairs seemed to be different shades of pine and on closer examination I realised the chairs were light oak, not pine at all. They were obviously not meant to be together as a set, until destiny had intervened at some point in their separate and chequered pasts. I had long ago accepted their mismatched partnership.

Helen's letters were spread out in front of me on said table. I was reading them over and over, as if by some form of magical connection between the lined notepaper and my brain, I would be able to absorb the emotions of their author at the time they were written. Reading the letters was also an attempt to calm myself down as the adrenalin high was making my body shake. Glenn wandered into the kitchen wearing double denim as usual with his glasses poking out of his breast pocket.

"I can't believe there's still 25 minutes to go, Glenn. Why has the last hour felt like four?"

He did not say anything. I knew he was worried about the huge step I was about to take but, being Glenn, I knew he would watch, listen and then make his mind up.

I nearly jumped out of my skin (what a strange expression that is and not even physically possible) when the phone suddenly rang. I panicked because it was too early, was he calling to cancel or was it something else? My heart was beating loudly in my chest and echoing in my ears when I picked up the shrill instrument, pressed the green button and said, "Hello."

"Hi, Mum, what time are you speaking to him?" It was my daughter, Amanda, calling.

"Oh, hi, love. He said he would call at 10:30. I'm not sure if I'm psyching myself up or down."

"It'll be fine, Mum, don't worry. Where's Dad?"

"He's here in the kitchen with me."

"Can I speak to him? I'll only be a few minutes. Call me later and let me know how it went."

"Sure. I'll call you later. Lots of love."

While they talked on the phone, I reflected on the developments of the previous five months that started with that first business trip to Edinburgh.

"Do you want a coffee?" The whistle of the boiling kettle and Glenn's question interrupted my thoughts.

"Yes please, what time is it?"

I rendered the question rhetorical by glancing at the large ship-style clock above the kitchen door. I had spotted the clock in the window of a gift shop during a wedding anniversary weekend in Stratford-upon-Avon and decided that I could not leave the city without it. The clock said 10:30, but I knew that meant 10:15. The clock was always set 15 minutes fast, a weird habit we had followed for many years. Maybe the original intention was to ensure that we were not late but as we always mentally deducted 15 minutes from the time displayed, any advantage was negated.

Another 15 interminable minutes later, I was fidgeting in front of the kitchen window overlooking our back garden. My coffee in my favourite 'I love my grandma' mug given to me by Chelsea, my first grandchild, on a Mothers' Day many years before, was sitting on the kitchen worktop in front of me. Although I was expecting the call, the ringing phone startled me. I took a deep breath and lifted the phone from its cradle next to the bread bin on the beige tiled worktop. I always made or took significant phone calls standing up – not sure why but maybe it made me feel more assertive. I glanced over my shoulder. Glenn had taken my place at the table, and he gave me a reassuring nod.

I pressed the green button on the ringing phone, my heart beating so loudly it was echoing in my ears and threatening to drown out any conversation.

I cleared my throat and said, "Hello."

"Carol?"

"Yes, is that William?"

"Aye, but my friends call me Billy."

The strong Glaswegian accent surprised me because I knew he had left Scotland in the early 1970s.

"I wasn't sure if you would sound Scottish or Australian but it's clear you've never lost your accent," I commented and smiled though he couldn't see me.

"We were wondering if you would have a Scottish or an English accent – you sound English." Billy sounded surprised.

"That's probably because my accent was never strong to start with and I moved to England nearly 40 years ago."

I heard a voice in the background with a distinctive Australian twang.

"Tommy is asking which football team you support, Carol?"

"Celtic," I replied quickly.

"That's great, so do I," Billy confirmed, "but unfortunately Tommy supports Rangers!" I heard a 'huh' in the background and assumed it came from Tommy.

"I guess having lived in England since 1970, you may have expected me to say a team like Manchester United or Chelsea, but my dad supported Rangers, and I remember teasing him at the start of the 1966-1967 football season by saying that I was going to support Celtic. When they won the European Cup in 1967,

I was hooked for life." I paused for a few seconds before asking, "Who did Helen support?"

"She was Celtic too. Tommy's the odd one out," Billy replied.

I heard whispering in the background, this time it sounded like a female voice. "Who else is with you, Billy, apart from Tommy?"

"Barbara and Linda"

I knew that Barbara was William-now-Billy's wife, that Linda was Billy's sister and my half-sister. Billy and Tommy were both my half-brothers.

At the age of 54, I was finally speaking with members of my birth family who, although they had not been aware of my existence until a few weeks earlier, sounded pleased to hear about me. It was like one of my childhood dreams, growing up as an only child and longing for siblings, had finally come to fruition. I turned round to Glenn with a huge smile on my face, but he just looked worried.

At that moment I knew I had to meet them face to face even although there were more than 10,000 miles between us!

We continued chatting for a few minutes about Billy's children, and the contents of both our letters.

I spoke briefly to Linda, Tommy and Barbara along similar lines, all safe topics about where they lived, worked, children, etc.

When Billy came back on the line, I decided to broach the matter of Ann. "Billy, are you in touch with Ann?"

I heard an intake of breath from Billy. "You know about Ann?"

"Yes, Violet told me that Ann was Helen's first baby and that she is in a wheelchair and lives in Australia."

"She had an accident at work and was in a wheelchair for a while but now she has crutches. Yes, we often see Ann and her family. She's married to John and has two daughters like you. Barbara put it together from your birthday, we think that you and Ann had the same father and are full sisters," Billy explained.

I was not expecting that, but that locked compartment in my mind evaporated and I felt both relieved and excited. Billy continued, "Barbara and I are going round to see Ann after this call and we'll tell her about you, I think it will be a bit of a shock to her."

"I would love to talk to her, Billy, will you let me know if she is willing to talk to me and if she is I'll call her in the morning."

Australia was 11 hours ahead of the UK so if I called early on Monday morning it would be early evening there. Barbara emailed me later to say that Ann was quite shocked but wanted to speak to me and she gave me her phone number.

I was walking on air for the rest of Sunday. Speaking to Billy and the others had been so easy and warm and then there was the imminent prospect of speaking to Ann who was probably my full sister. I planned to get up very early in the morning and call her. I shared all my news with my daughters, Tina and Amanda, and they were as excited as I was. Glenn was still being his usual cautious self.

We were watching TV that evening when the phone rang again for the umpteenth time that day. Glenn went into the hall and answered it. He came back into the lounge a minute later and simply said, "It's Ann," as he handed me the phone.

Chapter 14

Biochemistry, Hull,
September 1971–April 1972

I had to take two buses to get from our house to Hull Royal Infirmary where the Biochemistry lab was located. I was quite nervous on that first morning but hoped that this would be the start of a new direction and career for me. When I got to Hull Royal, as everyone called it, I reported to the front desk as directed and the receptionist told me where to go. I climbed the staircase adjacent to the four lifts in the foyer that took patients, staff, and visitors up to the wards. There were 13 floors but when I had been there for a while, I realised that there was no Ward 13. On each floor, the ward on the left was labelled as per the floor number and the ward on the right had the floor number multiplied by ten. So, on the sixth floor the ward on the left was Ward 6 and the ward on the right was Ward 60 but on the 13th floor the ward on the left was 130 West and the ward on the right was 130 East. Maybe the architect or someone on the Hospital Management Committee was superstitious.

That first morning I climbed the staircase and opened the two heavy wooden doors leading to the first-floor landing. Following the signs, I quickly reached a set of similar wooden doors at the entrance to the Biochemistry laboratory. I entered a long dark corridor with minimal overhead lighting and doors on either side, most of which were closed. The first thing that hit me was the pungent smell which I later came to realise was an unpleasant blend of blood, urine, faeces and the various chemicals and reagents required to perform tests on these bodily substances.

Keith Kemp, the chief technician, welcomed me, explained that I would be working on 'sugars' and introduced me to a small, bespectacled, and pregnant Pauline Field, who would show me what to do. After being shown my locker, I donned my brand new and pristine white lab coat and followed Pauline into the auto-analyser lab. This was a long narrow lab with three u-shaped bays and doors at each end leading to the main corridor. A metal tray stood on the workbench and Pauline told me it contained dark red venous blood in glass bottles that had come from the wards and the outpatient diabetic clinics. The bottles and their accompanying test request cards had been brought to the work bench by the lab porter, a cheerful Irish man called Sean.

'Sugars' involved labelling empty test tubes with sequential numbers and the name of the patient from the request card, placing the blood bottles in a centrifuge that spun them around dizzyingly to separate the serum from the red cells, and then transferring serum into the correspondingly numbered test-tube. That was the most unpleasant part, because in order to do that I had to put a pipette in the serum, place the other end in my mouth and suck it up it to the required level – a mark two thirds of the way up the pipette. I had been shown how to plug the top of the pipette with cotton wool but every time I did it,

I was worried that I would get some of the fluid in my mouth. Even worse, sometimes I had to do the same thing with urine. Apparently, in the Middle Ages physicians used to taste urine to help them diagnose certain conditions and I did not want to emulate them accidentally. So much for the glamour of being a scientist!

There was an even more unpleasant test in the same lab that thankfully I never had to perform and that involved reducing faecal fats (stools) over boiling benzene in a fume cupboard. We now know that benzene is a carcinogen but in 1971 it would be three more years until the Health and Safety at Work Act 1974 came into force, so these unsafe practices continued.

Having filled the test tubes, I then had to pour some of the serum from each one into a small plastic cup sitting beside the same number as the test tube in a circular tray on the auto-analyser machine. The tray rotated and the machine sucked up each sample and analysed the level of glucose in each one. The results were printed out and I had to write them onto the request card that accompanied the original glass blood bottle. The cards then went into the lab office for reporting to wards, departments or doctors before they were filed.

The blood did not always come in glass bottles, sometimes it came inside a person. On diabetic clinic days, outpatients came to the lab, and I extracted capillary blood from them by squeezing their thumb until it turned dark pink and then stabbing it with a small lancet. After the first control test, which was a fasting blood sugar, I gave the patient a glucose drink and then collected and tested his or her blood again at 30-minute intervals to see how well the individual was metabolising the glucose. This process usually took about three hours and there could be several patients on each of these mornings. I managed to smile afresh at each new patient's vampire joke.

Twice a week, I and another technician would do ward rounds and collect capillary blood from diabetic inpatients using lancets in the same way. The geriatric (or 'medical elderly', as they are known now) wards were the worst, not only because of the pervasive smell of incontinence, but sometimes a very confused patient, who did not understand what you were doing, would get upset or try to fight you off.

I had been in the lab for about two weeks when Chris Cox, one of the senior technicians, brought a different auto-analyser machine to my bench, set it up and showed me how to use it. The next morning when I arrived, there was a sarcastic note taped to the new machine. I can't remember exactly what it said but the gist was that the author was annoyed that I had not left information about the new auto-analyser. I was puzzled and showed it to Sharon who was working in the next bay. She told me that it was from Glenn who was on call overnight and was probably a bit pissed off that he was confronted with an unfamiliar machine. She said, "It's just Glenn being Glenn, ignore it!"

* * *

A few hours later, I saw a young man coming through the door at the other end of the lab, he looked quite fierce. He was tall and moving quickly so his open lab coat fanned out behind him like a whirling Dervish skirt. He had striking cornflower blue eyes and chin length dark brown hair which would be considered long now but in 1971 was relatively short. He had a loose side parting and a fringe that he kept out of his eyes by running his fingers through it as he approached. Long sideburns were fashionable at the time and his were lighter than his hair and close to being a full beard apart from a shaved area about an inch wide at his chin. He came up to me and said, "I'm Glenn, did you get my note?"

I blushed, something I did a lot in those days, apologised profusely, and explained that Chris Cox had changed the machine, and I had not been aware that I should leave a note for the on-call technician. I promised that if anything changed in the future, I would leave a note.

He nodded and the fierce expression disappeared. He said, "How's it going?"

"You mean working in the lab?" He nodded and I said, "Bit early to say, I've only been here two weeks."

He nodded again, turned abruptly and headed back to the door his lab coat flying out again. Most technicians wore their lab coats buttoned up, so I had not seen this phenomenon in the lab before.

I didn't see much of Glenn after that as he was working in the manual lab further down the corridor. Occasionally I would see him in the technician's room, a clean area where we had mid-morning and mid-afternoon breaks. He was usually either reading a fishing magazine by himself in a corner or chatting with one or more of the senior technicians, Chris Cox, Brian Baldwin, or Dave Beaumont.

We had to work one in seven Saturday mornings on a roster and one Saturday I was cleaning out the Astrup machine which was used to analyse blood gases.

The blood was fed into two glass tubes on the machine from a hypodermic needle and to clean the glass tubes you had to use alcohol-soaked cotton wool on the end of an orange stick (obviously a highly sophisticated procedure). As I was twisting the stick to clean the bottom of one of the glass tubes, the cotton wool came off. I tried and tried but I couldn't get it out of the bottom of the tube where it was lodged. Glenn came into the lab and saw what I was doing. He came over, picked up another orange stick, inserted it in the tube and with a deft flick of his hand, brought the cotton wool out. I thanked him and he left at a hundred miles an hour as before. I was embarrassed and annoyed with myself, this man probably thought that I was a complete idiot.

By February I was working on liver function tests in the manual lab, and I noticed that Glenn was now working in the automated lab on the SMA 3/60, a large machine capable of analysing urea and electrolytes at high speed on large volumes of serum samples. One day I was preparing some reagent for bilirubin testing when Glenn came into the manual lab and walked over to me. He said that Keith Kemp had told him I was Scottish, and he was thinking of going to Scotland in the summer with his brother. He had been to Edinburgh a few times but wondered if I could recommend somewhere else to visit. My brain went into a spin as I had not spent much time on the Scottish mainland, and I didn't want to look like an idiot in front of him again. Sudden inspiration saved me.

The year after Mum passed her driving test at her third attempt, the Loch Seaforth transported us and our little our Fiat 600 across the Minch, and she drove Daddy and me from Mallaig to Hull. It was probably summer 1966. Daddy came with us because Mammy did not want to drive all that way without him and because of that, it meant that we were only in Hull for just over two weeks rather than our usual longer stay. We had two overnight stops on the way, the first at Callander in Perthshire and the second one at Corbridge in Northumberland. A popular television series at the time was *Dr Finlay's Casebook*, set in the fictitious town of Tannochbrae. It was about two doctors, the younger, newly qualified and more impulsive Dr Finlay and the older, wiser and grumpier Dr Cameron. They lived and worked at Arden House with their long-suffering housekeep and receptionist, Janet. Although most of the series was shot in a studio, the exterior shots of Arden House were of a guest house in Calendar and on our way to Hull we had spent a night at the Arden House Guest House in Callander. I told Glenn about it, and he said he would check it out.

A few days later, Glenn approached me again and I assumed that he wanted to talk about Callander or Scotland so I was gobsmacked when he asked if I would like to go to the cinema with him the following evening, I said yes as calmly as I could, but inside I was buzzing.

Chapter 15

Ann
February 2009

As a child I had wished desperately for a sister and found out years later that I had been close to having a younger sibling, but Mum had a miscarriage when I was four. Now in less than 24 hours I had not only found out that I had a full sister, but I was about to speak to her. I was surprised but delighted that Ann had called me before I got round to calling her the next morning.

Like Billy, she had retained her Scottish accent but without the full Glaswegian dialect. She said that she had been shocked when Billy and Barbara had told her about me and although they said that I would call her the following day, she was so excited that she decided to call me as soon as the time difference allowed.

As Ann had read my letter to Billy, she went into our telephone conversation knowing much more about me than I did about her. So, I asked her to tell me all about herself. She told me she was married to John, had two daughter, Karen and Kristine, and a granddaughter called Chelsea. That was the first of many coincidences to follow because my first granddaughter was also called Chelsea. Ann told me that she had been engaged to someone else when she met John. She had arranged to go out with her friend, Margaret, and another girl,

Mary, who she did not really know. Margaret asked if Ann would mind if they didn't go out but went for a drink at Mary's house because her mother had just come out of hospital, and she didn't want to leave her alone. During the evening, Mary's brother, John, arrived but he had had a few drinks and asked Ann her name repeatedly. Initially she through he was very annoying but eventually he sobered up and asked if Ann would like to walk the dog with him. During that walk she realised that she really liked him. She broke off her engagement and three months later John proposed. They went to Manchester to find work and on 28th September 1973 they were married over there before returning to live in Glasgow.

* * *

Ann told me that although she grew up believing that Mary Ann and Wullie Blyth were her parents, she had always felt closer to Helen who she thought was her oldest sister. It was only after Ann was married and came back to Glasgow from Manchester with John that Helen told her the truth or rather part of the truth, as she had not told Ann about me. Helen had explained that she met a young English migrant called John Rankin when the family was in Australia, they fell in love and wanted to get married. Helen's mother, Mary Ann, would not agree to the marriage and as Helen was below the legal age of consent, they decided to get pregnant in the hope that it would force Mary Ann to change her mind. However, the plan backfired. When Mary Ann discovered that Helen was pregnant, she gave her the choice of having the baby adopted by strangers after it was born, or they (the grandparents) would bring the child up as though it was theirs. The second option was conditional on the fact that Helen must never tell the child that she was its true mother. Helen was powerless both legally and financially and chose the second option so that she could at least see the child growing up. Ann told me that the grandmother, Mary Ann, had always been called Nancy by old Wullie. Although all the family called her Ann, Helen had registered her birth name as Nancy, presumably as a way of trying to make a connection between her mother and her new baby in the hope Mary Ann would change her mind but that did not happen.

We discussed my adoption and surmised that Helen and John Rankin must have thought that if they became pregnant a second time, Mary Ann would have to give in and let them get married. Once again, they underestimated Mary Ann's determination and when she found out that Helen was pregnant again, she took the whole family back to Glasgow where I was born and subsequently adopted. Ann told me that John Rankin was heartbroken because the love of his life and his daughter (Ann) were at the other side of the world, and he had no money to go to the UK. He was so desperate that he tried to rob a bank at gunpoint but was caught. He only received a prison sentence of five years because there were no bullets in the shotgun he used. Ann knew that Helen and John kept in touch for years by sending letters through his auntie and that explained why Helen had said in the letters to Family Care that she could put me in touch with my natural father who would like to hear from me although they both married different people.

From Scotland's People, the official government source of genealogical information for Scotland, I was able to get a copy of Helen's birth certificate. She was born on 17th August 1934 so my original estimate of her age when she died was close. From the information given to me by Violet, I also got a copy of Mary Ann and Wullie's marriage certificate and was surprised to see that the date was 13th July 1934. Mary Ann was 18 years of age and almost eight months pregnant with Helen when they were married. Ann and I agreed that we could both accept that maybe Mary Ann had wanted Helen to have more choices in life and not be tied down with motherhood at a young age. What we found difficult to accept was that Mary Ann and Wullie had had three young children who had died, so they had personally experienced the pain of losing children and still made Helen go through that twice. Through Scotland's People I found that the children they had lost, Mary, Margaret, and Thomas had all died within a period of 18 months of each other during the Diphtheria epidemic that scourged Glasgow between 1934 and 1942. That also helped to explain the six-year age gap between Helen, who was born in 1934, and her brother, Tom, born in 1940. I thought it strange that a Thomas had died, and the same name was given to another child born later, but maybe it was viewed as an important family name as Wullie's father was named Thomas and I had come across this practice before in Uncle Donald's family.

* * *

From things she told me, it became apparent that Ann had not had a happy childhood. She referred to

Mary Ann as the 'Auldyin' and told me that she was strict, selfish, and parsimonious. Ann grew up in hand-me-down clothes from Violet, who was nine years older than her. However, when Caroline Blyth was born in 1958, she apparently got everything new which was divisive, and the two 'sisters' never formed a close relationship. Ann had independently come up with the same thought as Violet that the youngest daughter had been called Caroline to punish Helen because of the similarity of our names. She told me that she and Caroline had to sleep together in a curtained recess in the kitchen because Mary Ann rented out any spare bedrooms in the house to male lodgers. When Ann was in her teens, she had to take Caroline everywhere with her which cramped her style and when she was finally able to go out dancing, there would be rows at home if she missed the bus and came home late. On one occasion, Caroline had seen Ann kissing a boy in the back close and told Mary Ann. A huge row ensued, and Mary Ann threw some new clothes that Ann had bought with her savings onto the fire, the following day Ann had to go to work in one of Mary Ann's old dresses which came down to her shins. Ann hid her bank book and nylons in the outside toilet and the next day bought herself a suitcase, new clothes, and a ticket to London. She didn't like London and came back to Glasgow where her older 'brother' (really her uncle) Bill took her in and didn't tell Mary Ann that she was back. Houses had gas meters in those days, and with a filed-down key, Ann was able to take shillings out of the meter in Bill's house. When the gas man called to open the meter, he found it was empty and Bill called the police. Ann was sent to a remand home for a month and given six months' probation. At the home she and the other girls knitted small teddy bears that they could sell to friends and family to earn some money of their own. Helen and Wullie came to see her there and Ann remembers Wullie gave her a ten-shilling note. Once Ann came out of the remand home, Mary Ann sent her to live with Helen and Ann was very happy. However, Mary Ann or Wullie, at his wife's command, regularly checked up on Ann to ensure that she was compliant and that she was punished by Helen if she was not. Mary Ann was angry if Helen was not hard enough. Ann told me that she wished Helen had told her she was her mother when she went to live with her at age 15, because she would have behaved better to keep Mary Ann off Helen's back.

It seems that Wullie was a kinder person but completely under Mary Ann's thumb. He bet heavily on the horses and, from time to time, Ann or one of the other children had to take a note and items to 'Uncle Peter' at the local pawn shop without letting Mary Ann know what they were doing, and Wullie would give them money for doing that. He worked at the shipyards and sometimes brought home copper piping wrapped round his middle under his jacket and Ann would take this to the scrap merchants for him. He gave her money and once again she was told, "Shh, don't tell Mammy." Mary Ann had lovely jewellery and clothes that she kept in a locked wardrobe, but Wullie was able to open it with a knife and often pawned Mary Ann's personal possessions. If she noticed they were missing before he had chance to replace them, she would kick Wullie out of the house. Ann remembers sneaking him back in several times after it was dark, and he slept under her bed.

However, sometimes Wullie actually won money on the horses, and Ann told me that he had bet on Foinavon in the 1967 Grand National, an outsider who won with odds of 100/1 when he managed to avoid a pile up at the 23rd fence. When Wullie came home, he started throwing £5 notes up in the air and gave one to Ann. He also gave Helen a sum of money which allowed her to buy her first house.

By the time she was 16 years old, Ann couldn't stand living within Mary Ann's reach any longer and ran away for a second time. When she got to Glasgow Central Station, she saw that the next train to depart was the Manchester train, so she bought a ticket and waited on the platform. There she met another girl in the same boat as her, so they teamed up, found a flat together and started working in Manchester. She only came back to Glasgow twice and it was on the second of those occasions that she met John.

I reflected that both Ann and I had been separated from our birth mother and brought up by older parents, but I had fared significantly better than Ann growing up.

Our first phone conversation lasted for more than three hours as we both had voracious appetites to find out more about our full blood sister and although it is not easy to build a close relationship over the telephone, we managed to do just that very quickly. Until December 2008, I had assumed that my birth mother was in Glasgow, and it was shock to find out that my birth family were at the other side of the world. During conversations with my brothers and sisters, I had been told several times that I looked like Helen. I couldn't really see it in the photos of Helen as an adult but when Barbara sent me a photo of Helen in her early teens and

Me age 12 (left) and Helen early teens (right).

I compared it with one of me taken when I was 12 years old, I could see some resemblances in our facial features, particularly our eyes, noses and chins.

* * *

The more telephone conversations I had with Ann and the others, the more I realised that just finding out information about Helen, Ann, Billy, Linda, and Tom, was not enough. I had a desperate need to meet them and soon; none of us were getting any younger. I started working on a plan for Glenn and I to go to Melbourne later in the year, after the Australian winter ended. I knew Glenn would be hesitant and see all the downsides before the benefits in his usual 'glass half-empty' style so I started to formulate arguments I could use to address the concerns I knew he would raise.

Chapter 16

Migration to Australia
1951, 1974 and 1982

At the end of the Second World War, the population of Australia was 7.5 million and as part of its 'populate or perish' policy the Australian government introduced an Assisted Passage Migration Scheme in 1945 to encourage British families to emigrate to Australia to assist post-war reconstruction and drive economic growth. In return for subsidising the cost of travel, they promised good employment prospects and affordable housing. Children travelled free of charge and the adult fare was £10. Those who took advantage of the scheme became known as 'Ten Pound Poms', and large numbers of Scottish and Irish families migrated as well as English ones. The scheme was also open to British colonies like Eire, Malta and Cyprus. The deal was that they had to stay for two years, or they would have to refund the fares. Initially migrants had to be under 45 years of age and in good health, and at that time there was no skill requirement but as the scheme developed migrants were expected to have a trade or some specialist skills to be able to contribute to the Australian economy.

The Australian administration wanted to perpetuate the values and culture of Britain and the Commonwealth in Australia, and it was believed that Britons would settle easily and quickly due to the shared language and similar culture.

Arthur Caldwell, the first minister for immigration, wanted an immigration ratio of ten Britons to every one of other nationalities but after the first migrant rush he set a new aspirational target of Britons being 50% of all migrants.

Over a million Britons migrated to Australia between 1945 and 1972. In 1951 the Assisted Package Scheme was extended to the Netherlands and Italy, in 1952 to Greece and West Germany and in 1967 to Turkey.

* * *

Mary Ann and Wullie had four children when they emigrated to Australia in 1951, Helen was the eldest and was 17 when they made the journey, Tom was the second eldest at 11, Bill was 9 and Violet was 7. Sadly Helen, Tom and Bill have all died and Violet was so young that she has only sketchy memories of Australia and their passage over there in 1951 and the journey back home in 1954.

It is understandable why the family decided to take up the Assisted Package Scheme. Glasgow in the 1950s was not a pleasant place to live with emissions from domestic coal fires leading to severe smog in the densely populated city. Ironically, the Gaelic name for Glasgow is 'Glaschu' which means Green Glen! The smog and emissions caused the beautiful Georgian architecture built from red, beige, and grey sandstone to become caked in soot and Glasgow was often described by commentators as a dirty city.

In addition, there was the city's long history of violence which came to a peak in the 1920s and 1930s with the violent razor gangs based in the East End and South Side of Glasgow whose weapon of choice was the old cutthroat folding razor. These gangs were not only territorial but also sectarian. Glasgow had been a protestant city but in the 19th and 20th centuries large numbers of Catholic Irish immigrants came to the city searching for work. After the great depression of the 1920s, unemployment in Glasgow escalated. Between 1930 and 1935 it was running between 25% and 33% and jobless young men found focus and purpose in street gangs. This situation improved due to the Second World War as many of these young men were drafted. However, in the early 1950s, new, younger, and even more violent gangs started to surface although they were subdued to a degree by a particular Glasgow Judge called Lord Carmont who handed out extremely heavy sentences. Glasgow's reputation for violence was also reflected in popular culture through the widely understood 'Glasgow Kiss', a sudden head-butting action designed to break an opponent or victim's nose and the 'Glasgow Smile' where a victim's face was cut from the mouth to the ear on each side leaving a scar that looked as though the individual was smiling much like Joaquin Phoenix in *Joker*, the award-winning 2019 film. The difference was that the character voluntarily did it to himself.

Football was a highly public manifestation of sectarian violence and conflict between Protestant supporters of Rangers and Catholic supporters of Celtic. City centre battles between football hooligans on both sides were legendary.

There may have been many other factors contributing to the Blyth family's decision to emigrate to Australia as Ten Pound Poms in 1951 as well as the violence and smoggy atmosphere in post war Glasgow but sadly I will never know the exact reasons. The scheme welcomed ex-servicemen and as Wullie had been in the army in World War II, maybe the heavily subsidised scheme proved attractive to him and his family as an opportunity to start a new life 'down under'.

I found from ship manifests that they travelled on the SS *Cameronia,* a three-class ocean liner originally built in Glasgow in 1920 for the Anchor Line which was owned by Cunard. Originally it had accommodation for 265 first class passengers, 370 second class passengers and 1100 third class passengers. During World War II she was used as a troop carrier and landing ship, and she took part in the allied invasion of North Africa in 1942. In 1948, still under the ownership of the Anchor Line, she underwent a refit to become a single-class liner with accommodation for 1,266 passengers and was used to transport people migrating to Australia. On their return journey in 1954, the Blyth family travelled on the SS *Fairsea.*

Stories from migrants in the 1950s and 1960s reflect very different experiences influenced strongly by the facilities on their ship, and relationships with fellow passengers. In an article entitled 'Journey to Australia', published by the Immigration Museum in Victoria, one person who migrated from Hungary in 1951 said, "The *Fairsea* was huge, a converted troop ship with no cabins just huge, big open spaces with triple decked bunks, so cramped you couldn't sit up straight in them. Men were assigned to one section, women to the other. The toilet and shower facilities were one huge, long one and everywhere you went there was an awful reek of 'White King'. People threw up because of the smell not just the swell!"

The open spaces he described were empty ship holds hastily converted into single sex dormitories and in another article, I found out that White King was a brand of bleach. Later migrants on more modern passenger liners described the month-long journey as the cruise of a lifetime.

The Blyth family arrived in Freemantle, Western Australia in December 1951 according to Australian National Archives. At some point they moved to the Melbourne area in South-East Australia because Helen told Billy and Barbara that the family settled in Altona which is a suburb of Melbourne located approximately 13 miles south-west of the city centre. Altona experienced significant population growth since that time due to the expansion of the petrochemical industry and high levels of British and European immigration. In 1954 when the Blyth family returned to Glasgow, Altona's population was 6,698, in 2016, the year of the last national census, the figure recorded was 10,762.

Helen told Billy and Barbara that there was extensive farmland near where they stayed. In 1961, seven years after the Blyth family repatriated, Altona Memorial Park was opened and now covers a large proportion of the former farmland. Helen is buried in Altona cemetery, close to where the family lived in the early 1950s, and her grave lies less than 100 metres from Wullie and Mary Ann's graves.

* * *

Due to her mother's decision to repatriate the whole family, Helen left Australia in early 1954 but came back again with her husband and children in 1974. It was not unusual for migrants to return to the UK and then go back to Australia later. They became known as 'Boomerang Poms'.

After buying her first house with money from Wullie's winnings, Helen did the house up and sold it for a profit, she then bought another one and did the same thing. She continued to repeat the process of buying, improving and selling properties with the objective of saving enough money to go back to Australia. Billy said that growing up they felt like gypsies because they were always moving to a new house. In 1974 Helen and my half-sister, Linda, travelled to Australia to find work and send money back to allow the rest of the family to migrate. Linda recalled that they sailed from Southampton on the SS *Australis*. From Wikipedia I discovered that the vessel was built in the United States in 1940 as a large and luxurious North Atlantic passenger liner but by the time she was ready for her maiden voyage, the war situation in Europe was so unstable that she was diverted to Pacific cruises instead. In 1941 the liner was requisitioned by the Maritime Commission and became the USS *West Point*, at that time the US Navy's largest troop carrier. When the Second world War ended, she became SS *Australis* again and continued to carry passengers between the United States and Europe until the bottom fell out of transatlantic liner market as passengers were increasingly choosing to fly. In 1964 she was sold to the Chandris Shipping Line in Greece who had won the lucrative Australian Migrant contract. After a refit at their yard in Piraeus that converted the three-class accommodation to a single-class, increasing its passenger capacity from 1,046 to 2,300 she started her new role transporting migrants from Europe to Australia. To migrants travelling on the refitted *Australis*, it must have felt like a luxurious journey. The liner had two swimming pools, a cocktail bar, coffee shops, a cinema, chemist's shop, a ballroom, two restaurants and each day the newsletter, *Seascape*, would publicise the events for the day including judo, bingo, 5-a-side football, chess, whist, needlework group, wrestling, canasta, and entertainment like 'Cocktails and Piano Keys' with Dennis.

I asked Linda if they had gone as 'Ten Pound Poms', but she said no, they had to pay. Helen had told Billy and Barbara that she was not accepted for the Assisted Passage Scheme in 1974 because her husband, Sammy, did not have a trade. I discovered that the fare for the Assisted Package Scheme had increased from the original £10 to £75 in 1973 which would be equivalent to over £1200 in 2024, so Helen and Linda would have had to pay significantly more to realise Helen's dream of returning to Australia.

When Helen and Linda arrived in Melbourne, they found factory work together and set about saving as much money as they could. They stayed in a room in a boarding house opposite the beach in St Kilda with a communal bathroom but no access to a kitchen so they would go out for a walk after work and buy fish and chips. There was no television in the room so in the evenings they sat and listened to the radio.

They spent as little as they could on rent, food and travel to work and sent as much money as they could back to the family in Glasgow. Sammy, Tommy and Stevie were able to fly to Australia a few months later but Billy stayed in Glasgow to finish his bricklaying apprenticeship before emigrating. The family rented a house in Toorak, an inner suburb of Melbourne. Wullie, Mary Ann, and Caroline also migrated to Australia later in 1974 and lived close by. They were also boomerang poms and made return trips between Glasgow and Melbourne on at least three occasions.

In July 1974, Helen was admitted to hospital with gallstones and Wullie loaned Billy the air fare to visit her in Melbourne. Helen was pleased to have her family together again and persuaded Billy to stay and give Australia a chance for two years. He complied with her wishes but by the end of the two-year period, Billy had already decided that he wanted to go back to Glasgow. He had met Barbara by then, and they returned to Scotland together and were married in Glasgow in April 1977. Helen was not pleased that they decided to leave Australia.

In 1977, Helen decided to take the whole family back to Glasgow again, unfortunately I cannot ask her why. She was very close to Billy so maybe that was a factor. Also, I was told that allegedly she had been involved in a fight with a woman and the woman had lost the sight in one eye, so the possibility of criminal charges may also have influenced her decision. Sammy, Tommy, and Stevie flew from Australia to Glasgow, but Helen and Linda arrived by ship just a few days after Billy and Barbara's wedding. The Hudson family moved into a council house but life in Glasgow in 1977 was tough and soon Helen realised that her children would have a better life in Australia so took them back again. Before she returned to Australia, she gave Billy £1,000 to cover two one-way air tickets to Australia in the hope that he and Barbara would return at some point and made him promise that he would not use the money for anything else.

Billy and Barbara tried hard to make it work in Glasgow after Helen returned to Australia, but it was a tough time for them. Billy managed to find work, but Barbara couldn't and trying to survive on a single wage against a background of crippling inflation was a struggle. Inflation in the UK was running at 6.37% in 1970 but by 1974, the year the Hudson family migrated, it had increased to 16.04% because of consumer demand in the UK exceeding supply and the cost of oil from the Middle East quadrupling in price, following the Arab members of OPEC's oil embargo due to the Arab-Israeli war. In 1975, inflation hit a record high of 24.24% and in 1976 the value of the pound fell to a record low against the US dollar leading to the sterling crisis which forced Callaghan's government to borrow $3.9 billion from the International Monetary Fund, the largest loan ever issued. Inflation was running at 15.85% when Billy and Barbara rented rooms in Glasgow where the rent alone took up half of Billy's weekly wage. They wanted to start a family but when they looked at prams in Mothercare they realised that they cost three weeks wages. Barbara's family were originally from Manchester, but her mother had died in late 1976 and her body had been shipped back to Manchester to be buried with Barbara's grandmother. Barbara's aunt, cousin and grandfather lived in Manchester so they investigated moving to that city, but Billy could not find employment there. Barbara felt very torn, Helen wanted them to go back to Australia and she wanted to stay in the UK to be closer to her family. She adored her grandfather, and he was the one who finally helped Barbara to make up her mind. He took her to her mother's grave and told Barbara that her mother didn't like being away from the family, but she believed that her family would have a better life in

Australia. He said, "Don't let it all be for nothing." He simply wanted the best for Barbara and Billy and saw they had a chance to have a good life together in Australia.

I can understand how difficult the family separation must have been for both Helen and Barbara because the distance between the UK and Australia was so great and the cost of getting there prohibitive in that era.

Billy and Barbara finally decided to return to Melbourne and arrived home on 17th August 1977, on Helen's birthday. It must have seemed like the best birthday present ever.

***

In 1982, Ann and John were living in Glasgow. She was managing a local pub, John was a forklift truck driver, Karen was eight years old, and Kristine was four. Helen had tried several times to persuade Ann and family to go to Australia for a holiday and offered to loan them money for the air tickets. Although she missed Helen and the family, Ann had not given this any serious consideration. One evening, she and John went out for a drink and Australia came up in their conversation. Suddenly John said, "Ask Helen if she'll loan us the money for flights and we'll all go there." He was not talking about a holiday but moving there and Ann assumed it was the drink talking. The next morning, she asked him if he remembered what he had said the night before and he said, "About going to Australia, yes." Ann was born in Australia and had an Australian passport, so she was able to get her daughters Australian passports with dual citizenship. They knew it would take longer to find their way through the bureaucracy to get the necessary approvals and entry documents for John, so they decided that Ann and the girls would go first, and John would join them as soon as his application was approved. On 19th June 1982, which was Kristine's fifth birthday, Ann, Karen and Kristine flew out of Heathrow Airport on a Philippine Airlines flight to Australia.

I asked Ann about her first impression of Melbourne, she said it was not as exotic as she had envisaged, and the weather was disappointing because they had arrived at the start of the Australian winter. I had seen the posters used as part of the 'populate or perish' campaign and they all displayed wonderful images of families enjoying sun, sea and sand. I wondered if some of the early migrants entranced by those images also felt disappointed when they arrived in Southern Australia in winter. It took John seven and a half months to get the necessary approvals to join them and he finally arrived in February 1983. Ann sent me a photograph of her family taken on the day they were finally reunited, and I was staggered by the resemblance between Kristine and my daughter, Tina. A few days later I showed it to my sisters-in-law, Kay and Bridget who had married Jon, with my hand covering the rest of Ann's family and asked who the little girl was. They both said "Tina".

Chapter 17

Glenn and I
1971–1972

When Glenn asked me to go to the cinema with him, I was already seeing someone, but I thought that one cinema visit with a work colleague wouldn't do any harm.

In July 1970, I was at Uncle Ken's house waiting for his friend, Malcolm, to arrive as we were all going to see the Incredible String Band. I don't know what I was expecting but I was pleasantly surprised; he was in his late 20s, not in his 50s as I had assumed, and he was divorced. He was very tall and slimly built with brown hair in a James Dean-type hairstyle and bright blue eyes. Uncle Ken, Malcolm and I shared a love of music and for a while the three of us spent time together either at live gigs or sitting in Uncle Ken's music room, a converted bedroom, where he would play either his electronic organ or acoustic guitar, Malcolm would play his 12-string guitar, and I would sing. One thing led to another, and Malcolm and I started seeing each other in late October 1970. This was a bone of contention with Mum who thought he was 'very clean', but she was not impressed that he worked at the trade counter in FR Scott's Ironmongers. We didn't have much in common apart from music, but he was good to me, restored some of my self-confidence and, on reflection, maybe I was looking for a father figure.

Glenn had asked for my address and as film listings changed each Thursday, said he would have look at what was on and pick me up. I don't think he mentioned a time, but in my head, I expected he would come around 7:00pm, that was the time Malcolm usually came to pick me up and when you started doing things in the evening.

That Thursday evening, I took time and particular care over my make up and put on my nicest outfit, a yellow satin blouse, a brown suede skirt and matching suede boots. I was ready well before 7:00pm, but he did not appear. I waited and waited and around 8:00pm I concluded that he had changed his mind, and why not, I was amazed that he had asked me out in the first place.

I dispiritedly changed into jeans and a jumper and went into the front room to see what was on the telly. The three-bedroomed terraced house that Mum had bought on Summergangs Road was a similar design to Grandma Trowell's house but it was slightly bigger and thankfully had a bathroom upstairs and hot water. The television was in the front room along with the brown three-piece suite from Stornoway that was now green due to transformational slip-on covers. I had just opened the *Radio Times* when the front doorbell rang. I opened the door and Glenn was standing there. He had on a grey flecked fisherman's jumper, wine-coloured flared jeans, brown boots and a green parka with a fur-edged hood.

He said, "The programme starts at 8:30pm so we just have just enough time to drive to town and park up."

I explained that I needed to change but he said that I looked fine. I conceded; after all, he was dressed casually too. We got into the ABC Cinema five minutes before the adverts and trailers started. He went to the kiosk and asked what I wanted. I was about to say, "Nothing, thank you," when I saw him picking up bags of wine gums and fruit pastels. I told him that wine gums would be great.

Well, how can I describe Ken Russell's *The Devils*? It certainly was not a safe option for a first date as it was full of debauchery, nudity, nuns and priests having sex.

When he took me home in his white minivan, I asked him in for coffee. Because the film had started late it also finished late so Mum was in bed. He said that he didn't really drink coffee, so I made tea for him and a coffee for me. We sat in the back room for at least two hours, and I learned a lot about him. He was nearly five years older than me and had two brothers, Howard, who was two years older, and Jon, who was four years younger, his mother was a housemother at Hesslewood Orphanage and his father worked in the salaries department at Victoria House which was part of the hospital group. He told me that he had lived in Preston as a young child and loved being there and attending the village school. His family relocated to Hornsea in 1959, and he felt that he had gone backwards because during his first year they covered all the work he had done the previous year in Preston School. From there he had gone to Bridlington Grammar School, and he had hated his time there. He achieved seven O-levels then left school and joined Biochemistry. He had started in the lab in the old infirmary on Prospect Street before it moved to the new hospital when it opened in 1967.

I found he was easy to talk to and had a wicked sense of humour. I was still seeing Malcolm and although I still did not know Glenn very well, I knew I had to choose between them and without hesitation chose Glenn.

* * *

We started hanging out at lunchtime and frequently went into the city centre to pick up sandwiches and crisps. We drove to Pearson Park or West Park, both only a few minutes' drive from the hospital and depending on the weather we either ate the food sitting in his white minivan or on a bench under trees that were starting to bud.

He took me to Hesslewood Orphanage before we went out one evening and I briefly met his mother, Marie, his father, Jack, his brother, Jonathan (Jon), Pip, the family dog, and Glenn's ferrets – he had two and I found out the hard way that they had extremely sharp teeth. He told me that when he lived in Hornsea he had a ferret called Ruby who was quite big and fat and sometimes he and his brother, Jon, would take her for a walk on a collar and a lead. One old lady had a narrow escape when she bent down to pat 'this lovely dog' but Glenn had managed to pull Ruby away before she went for the lady's hand.

He belonged to the Hospital Fresh Water Angling Club and told me he was going to the Hospital Pond at Market Weighton one Saturday afternoon and would I like to go. I wanted to spend time with him so of course I said yes but watching him put wriggling maggots on to a hook to catch the perch and roach in there was a bit icky.

On 31st March, which was Good Friday, he suggested going up to the North Yorkshire moors. I had never been in that area so was interested to see what it was like. He took me up to Fylingdales and past three enormous white domes standing proud of the moor which he told me were a ballistic missile early warning system nicknamed the 'golf balls". We picked up some lunch from a small grocery shop and ate it in the car because it was cold and raining intermittently. Glenn took the foil top off a hazelnut yogurt and put the pot on the central console between us just as I moved my arm and inadvertently knocked it over onto his jeans. He shouted at me and called me stupid. I was shocked and upset because shouting was not something we did in my family but then I was angry because he should not have put the open yogurt pot there in the first place. I opened the minivan door and stormed off into the middle of nowhere and kept walking away from the parked car. I had no idea where I was or in which direction I was going, but I kept on walking. Glenn drove alongside me with the window down and told me to get back in the car. I shook my head and carried on walking. I had no clue what I was going to do but I was furious. Eventually he stopped the car, got out, came over to me and said, "I'm sorry, please get back in the car." So, I did.

* * *

There were no more spillages or shouting and we quickly got over the incident. Only a few weeks later he suggested moving in together. I was only three months away from my 18th birthday and legally becoming an adult, and I thought it was a great idea. However, Mum was not happy and the relationship between her and Glenn was very strained.

We started looking for somewhere to live and were surprised that in 1972 we found that some landlords were reluctant to rent to a couple who were not married. Eventually we found a furnished yellow brick Victorian terraced house to rent at 114 Albert Avenue, just off Anlaby Road and only a short distance from Hull Royal, that we could move into straightaway. We knew this was a temporary situation as the owner was abroad for three months, but that would give us time to find something more permanent.

The week before we moved in, I left Biochemistry. I had decided in February before Glenn asked me out that it was not the right kind of work or environment for me and started looking for a new job. I applied successfully for a clerical position in the health department which was based in the Guildhall in Hull, and I started my new job on 2nd May 1972. Although I missed working with Glenn, we were together in the house in the evenings and weekends unless he was on call. He drove me to the Guildhall every morning, met me for lunch and picked me up after work. I had to wait for him because we both finished work at five o'clock and he had to navigate through the heavy city centre traffic at rush hour but that didn't matter.

The work at the health department turned out to be quite boring but at least I didn't have to deal with the obnoxious bodily fluids and lab smells any more. My job title was clerical assistant which meant that I was a receptionist and office junior. I had to deal with visitors and enquiries from the public over a counter at the entrance, run errands, make tea and coffee and wash the cups up afterwards in the ladies toilet downstairs (looking back, that was not a very healthy practice in a health department), put letters into envelopes and deliver them to related public health and environment departments in the old town area of Hull. I also had to make multiple copies using a Gestetner duplicating machine. One of the typists would type a letter or information update onto a stencil, I would fit this stencil onto the drum of the machine and remove the top layer to reveal the heavily inked sheet underneath. When I turned the handle on the machine, the drum would rotate and roll over sheets of paper automatically fed through the tray underneath imprinting the content of the stencil on the paper. This allowed us to make multiple copies of the same document in the days before photocopiers. It was a very messy business; more than one blouse sleeve became inked, and it was tiring on the arm if I had to reproduce a high volume of copies. Twice a week we had a treat because Percy Pantry, the health department delivery driver, came to the office. He was short, chubby and wore a uniform similar to ambulance drivers at that time and he was always jovial. He brought Walnut Whips for the four of us based in the general office, two plain chocolate and two milk chocolate ones. We all preferred the milk chocolate ones, but you don't look a gift horse in the mouth, so we alternated, meaning that we all had a milk chocolate Walnut Whip once a week.

Glenn and I would often go to his family's apartments at Hesslewood Orphanage, and I got to know his parents, Marie (pronounced Marry) and Jack, along with his brothers, Howard and Jon, who Marie called Jonathan. Glenn and Jon often played snooker in the snooker room behind the apartment. I couldn't play but I used to like to sit there and watch them. I saw a lot more of Jon than Howard but one day I met Howard's girlfriend, Kay, whose mother was also a housemother at the orphanage although the family did not live on site. Howard worked in an administration job at British Aerospace in Brough and Kay worked in the main TSB bank in Hull. One lunchtime, Glenn took me to meet his maternal grandmother, 'Nan Ras' as she was called, in her small two-up two-down terraced house on Glasgow Street which runs between Selby Street and Woodcock Street and is close to Anlaby Road in Hull. Glenn seemed very fond of his nan and helped her make a pot of tea. Although I didn't like tea, I felt that I could not refuse when she offered. Her hands shook dramatically and when she sat talking to us drinking her tea from her china cup, I was worried that the tea would come over the side of the cup and scald her, but she managed admirably.

Nan Ras's maiden name was Lilian Stone, and she was born and grew up in Hull. In January 1917 she married Peder Rassmussen, a Norwegian seaman. They had Marie and four sons, Gerald, Alec, Peter, and Rolf. Peder died in October 1947, aged 63 from a chronic lung disease which was a legacy from being torpedoed early in the war and having to swim in contaminated water. Gerald and Peter still lived in Hull, Alec had emigrated to Australia after the war and sadly Rolf had died as a young man at the age 26 from a congenital condition.

I found out that Glenn's paternal grandmother's family was originally French. Zitella was born in Hull in 1890, married John William Marshall in 1912 and gave birth to four sons, George, Cyril, Jack and Leonard, and a daughter, Phyllis, but I gathered that Glenn's relationship with Nanna Marshall was not as close as with Lilian. I must admit I found Glenn's diverse heritage very interesting.

* * *

Although we were taking precautions, in July shortly before my 18th birthday, I discovered that I was pregnant. We were both quite shocked. Glenn said that we ought to get married but although I was scared about the idea of having a baby, I thought it was too soon to make a commitment as big as marriage and I didn't like the idea of a shotgun wedding. I remember saying, "No let's wait and see until after the baby is born."

We had been looking for new accommodation and found an upstairs unfurnished flat in a large yellow brick Victorian terrace house, 36 Glencoe Street, quite close to Albert Avenue but on the other side of Anlaby Road. It had a large living room with an antique fireplace, one bedroom with a ugly built-in wardrobe, a reasonable sized kitchen with a gas cooker, and a bathroom. The living room and bedroom were carpeted but the main staircase was not, so you could always tell when someone was coming up the stairs. We had no furniture, so we had to get some essentials quickly. By the time we moved in, Glenn had found a second-hand kitchen table and chair set in *Hull Daily Mail's* miscellaneous sales columns. We bought a bed, bedding, towels and everything we needed to be able to cook and eat in the kitchen. We had no seating for the living room, so we either sat in the kitchen or alternatively we sat on the floor in the living room listening to music. I had brought my grey and blue two-tone record player that Daddy had bought me, and between us we had a great supply of records including some duplicates, namely *Disraeli Gears* by Cream and Cat Steven's *Tea for the Tillerman*. I remember us sitting on cushions on the floor listening to Cat Stevens' *Teaser & the Firecat* and Carole King's *Tapestry* LPs. We often played Don McLean's *American Pie* album, all the songs were brilliant, but I particularly loved 'Winterwood' and 'Empty Chairs'.

We soon decided to buy some seating and found a three-piece L-shaped orangey-brown seating unit in a sale in a furniture shop on Spring Bank West which did the job, and we decorated the room to match. We also decorated the kitchen with white wallpaper covered in red boxes about twelve inches apart with a green stick at the top of the box. The first time Glenn's dad, Jack, came into the kitchen, he laughed and pointed out that the boxes were supposed to represent flowers, and we had hung the wallpaper upside down. We decided we liked it that way.

There was a young man in the downstairs flat. We saw very little of him, but he obviously liked the singer, Melanie, who was popular at the time because we often heard her voice murdering the Rolling Stones' 'Ruby Tuesday' or warbling through 'I've got a brand-new key'.

* * *

We didn't tell Glenn's parents about the pregnancy, but we spent a lot of time in their apartments at Hesslewood and Marie guessed. I saw Mum occasionally, but she was unaware of my condition. The worst part was the morning sickness and for a few weeks when I was working at my desk mid-morning the nausea would sweep over me and I had to get down the Guildhall's grand sweeping staircase to the ladies toilet on the ground floor as quickly as possible. Glenn still met me for lunch every day and on one occasion in Willis Ludlow's café, the smell of fish and cooked vegetables turned my stomach requiring a quick dash to the toilet there too.

I had always loved coffee; during the pregnancy I couldn't stomach it but developed a passion for Coca-Cola. On reflection it was probably a caffeine substitute.

One day at work, June the office supervisor took me into Dr Dunlop's office as it was empty. Dr Dunlop was a tall cheerful Scot who was the medical officer of health (MOH). In a conspiratorial whisper, which was not necessary in an empty office, she asked, "Are you expecting?" I said that I was, and she asked me when the baby was due.

Nothing else was said that day, but the following day she told me that because of my condition, they were going to send me to work at another health department office in Witham, it was across the river in East Hull but only about five minutes by car. She made some noises about it being better for me not to have to carry trays of cups up and down the stairs every day, but it was obvious to me that having an unmarried pregnant girl dealing with the public would be an embarrassment. However, I was so happy when I got to Witham; it was a small friendly office dealing with cow's milk allergy tests for babies and the organisation of health clinics across Hull. I sat opposite a lovely lady called Penny and we stayed friends for a long time afterwards.

The 1975 Employment Act was three years away in the future which meant that if you were pregnant, you left work three months before your due date and there was no statutory right to return. I knew that I would have to leave the Witham office in December 1972, and we started to consider the financial implications of that.

* * *

On 23rd November, the week before Glenn's 23rd birthday, he asked me again about getting married. I had had more time to think about the future and this time I said yes. We were making a life together and I realised it would be better for the baby if we were married before it was born. We went to the register office on George Street the next day at lunchtime and made the arrangements. The marriage would take place at 2:00pm on Friday 1st December. On Saturday we went to Henry Lees & Sons jewellers on Whitefriargate for the exciting purpose of choosing our wedding rings. There were so many to choose from and I was attracted by some 18 carat gold rings that had intricate patterns engraved on them. The assistant showing us the rings told me that both 18 and 22 carat gold were soft metals, and the pattern would wear off over time. He explained that if I wanted a patterned ring it was advisable to choose 9 carat gold because it was a harder metal. I chose a lovely 9 carat ring with a delicate leaf pattern on it and Glenn chose a wide plain gold ring in the same carat. The assistant put them into separate small cream leather pouches and Glenn tucked them into the inside pocket of his green parka coat. I noticed him regularly patting the pocket as we walked through the city centre to the car park.

That evening we went to see Mum and when we said we were getting married the following week she was not particularly happy, especially about the fact that I was 'expecting' but she accepted that it was going to happen. Glenn and Mum had been wary of each other ever since we moved in together and the situation had not really improved.

Both Mum and I had been worried about telling Auntie Agnes that I was pregnant and getting married. She would probably refer to me as a 'poor soul'. Glenn took control and wrote to her and Uncle Donald to introduce himself and explain what was happening and she and Uncle Donald sent us a card and some money as a wedding gift with no recriminations. I expect that Uncle Donald had something to do with that.

* * *

Glenn's brother, Howard, and his girlfriend, Kay, were married in September 1972, and I wore a long dress with a cream, beige and brown flowered pattern, and a wide brimmed cream hat. The dress material was soft so although it had an empire line it was quite gathered at the front, and no one had guessed that I was pregnant. My bump was still quite small at five and a half months, so I intended to wear the same outfit to get married in.

Glenn and Me on Howard and Kay's Wedding Day.

I ordered a small bouquet of white roses and made a hair appointment for the morning of Friday 1st December. Mum had said that everyone could go back to her house for refreshments after the marriage ceremony.

I used to be a deadliner, a habit it has taken me decades to conquer. At times it had potentially serious consequences and our wedding day was nearly one of those times. Luckily, both Glenn and I got up early on Friday morning and I took the dress out of the clumsily built-in wardrobe in the bedroom and tried it on. Shock horror, I could not zip it up and even if I could have, it made the bump look much bigger than it was. I panicked but Glenn said he would take me to Hesslewood, and his mother would help me find something to wear.

Marie was a very capable woman, and she drove me to Dorothea Bell's boutique in Hessle as soon as it opened. It was a lovely shop and there were a few possibilities for me, but I settled on a long velvet dress in a rich brown colour. The sleeves were made of a sheer light brown fabric, but they had intense swirling patterns of rich brown velvet inlaid in them. I loved the dress, and it not only fitted well but it also concealed the bump. My panic started to subside. My hair appointment was at the salon in Hammonds in the city centre on the same floor as the toy section I had loved so much when I was younger. Marie drove me to Hammonds, and I got there 15 minutes early, so I spent the time browsing around the store.

My brown hair hung just below my shoulders at that time, and I asked the stylist to create soft curls that could tumble out below my hat. I knew that the beige hat I had worn to Howard and Key's wedding would go with my new dress. When she had finished, I thought that the curls were a bit tight, but she explained that they would drop during the day. I was not totally convinced but accepted the explanation as she was the expert. I collected my bouquet and was dismayed to see that there were more white gerberas than white roses. The florist had said that it would be the other way round, but it was too late to make a change.

I caught a bus home and as I was getting off at the stop nearest to Glencoe Street, I realised that it had started to rain heavily, and my coat didn't have a hood. I started to run the 150 yards between the bus stop and the flat, battling against an oncoming wind that seemed to get stronger by the minute and clutching onto my Dorothea Bell bag and my bouquet for dear life. By the time I reached the flat I was drenched, dishevelled, and despondent.

I entered the flat, started to cry, and said to Glenn, "I can't get married like this, my hair is a mess and it's raining."

He put his arms around me and said, "It'll be okay." As I took a deep breath to calm myself, I inhaled his familiar comforting smell of Old Spice.

I changed into my dress, sorted my hair as best I could in the circumstances and put on the hat I had worn to Howard and Kay's wedding. Glenn had changed into a burgundy velvet jacket, matching trousers, a pink shirt and a wine-coloured tie, he looked handsome, and I felt ashamed that I had told him I could not get married because my hair was a mess. He had arranged for his dad to take us to the registry office in his cream Fiat 128. When they arrived to pick us up, I could see that Marie was carrying her fur coat and before we left the flat, she put it round my shoulders and said that I should wear it because it was so cold.

We arrived at the registry office a few minutes late, but it was not a problem. I saw all our relatives waiting; Mum, Uncle Ken and Auntie Doris, Auntie Joyce, my cousin, Lesley, with Rachel who was a baby, Nan Ras, Nanna Marshall, Phyllis (Jack's sister) Mrs Bays (Uncle Ken's mother), Uncle Billy (Mum's uncle), Kay and Jon. Howard had not been able to get the time off work.

The actual marriage ceremony is a blur; I remember my hands shaking as I put the ring on Glenn's finger and only know that we signed the register because I have a photo of us doing it. The clearest memory I have is when the photographs were being taken afterwards outside in the garden adjacent to the registry office. Luckily the rain had stopped temporarily but the wind that I had experienced running down Glencoe Street had increased to almost gale force proportions and I almost lost my hat several times. In more than one photo I am holding on to it and you can see that my dress is also being blown about. Marie had organised the photographer and it was only when we saw the photographs two weeks later that we realised that they were in black and white. So instead of the photos showing my brown velvet dress and Glenn's burgundy velvet suit, we looked as though we were both dressed in black.

Our Wedding Day.
Left to Right: Jack, Kay, Jon, Marie, Phyllis, Nan Ras, Glenn, me, Nanna Marshall, Uncle Billy, Mum, Uncle Ken, Auntie Doris, Lesley with baby Rachael, Mrs Bays, Auntie Joyce.

Back at Mum's house with sandwiches, sherry, and beer for the men, I saw Glenn whispering to Jon and the two of them disappeared for about half an hour. It transpired that he had decided to get some money out of the bank so we could go away for two-nights as a sort of spontaneous mini honeymoon. There were no ATMs in those days and banks closed at 3.30pm and he told me later that they had got to the bank in Jon's mini with about three minutes to spare. Through directory enquiries he found Southlands Hotel in Scarborough and booked us in for two nights. Jack drove us back to Glencoe Street to collect Glenn's minivan and we hastily packed and set off for Scarborough. It was very late and cold when we arrived and I remember us sitting in the lounge in front of a real coal fire, drinking milky coffee. I looked at the ring on my left hand and couldn't believe I was really married.

The resident fishing rod in the back of the van had come along too, so the next morning Glenn was fishing off Scarborough harbour and nearly hooked a fishing boat. Later we went for a meal and then on to the cinema and watched a film called *Klute* starring Donald Sutherland and Jane Fonda. Afterwards we went to the Lowenbrau Bier Keller, but we passed on standing on the benches and swinging tankards while the oompah band played. In those times there were no warnings about not drinking during pregnancy and we were both a bit drunk when we tried to find our way back to the hotel.

So overall our wedding was a very modest affair, no white wedding dress and veil, no bridesmaids, reception, wedding cake, speeches, or a first dance to our special song. During my 60th birthday party at the Hallmark Hotel in Hessle, I shared that with our guests and invited Glenn to have a first dance with me to what I regarded as our special song although we had never acknowledged it as such, Shania Twain's 'You're still the one'. Glenn and I had our 'first dance' 42 years after our wedding.

Chapter 18

Helen
1934–1996

During the telephone conversations with my newly found brothers and sisters, I was able to find out much more about Helen than she had included in her letters. I spoke to Linda occasionally but more frequently to Billy, Ann, and Tommy. I gained the strong impression from all of them that Helen adored her children and grandchildren, and it was apparent that they all adored her too and still missed her terribly 13 years after she had passed away.

She had grown up in what seemed to have been a very dysfunctional family ruled by Mary Ann and the relationship between Helen and her mother was complicated. Despite forcing Helen to give up two babies, Ann remembers Helen and Mary Ann often going shopping together, both pushing prams because Linda and Caroline were the same age. Also, Mary Ann had followed Helen and Sammy when they migrated to Australia in 1974, and the two families lived close to each other in St Kilda. Ann told me about a time in Australia when she and Helen went to visit Mary Ann in hospital and Helen confided in her that, despite being a grown woman with a family, she was 'shit-scared' of visiting her mother. Tommy's take on it was that, as the eldest, Helen couldn't do anything right. However, Violet left home and married young to get away from her 'mammy', Ann left home to get away from her too and over the years Mary Ann fell out with every one of her children. She didn't attend any of her children's weddings although she may have attended an informal reception in Kelvin Grove after her son Bill's marriage. After old Wullie died from a heart attack, Mary Ann became increasingly reliant on her youngest daughter, Caroline, particularly after she had her legs amputated. Mary Ann had been diagnosed with type 1 diabetes late in life but did not look after herself. By that time Caroline was married with a young son, but Mary Ann expected Caroline to push her everywhere in her wheelchair and Caroline did her bidding. This continued even after Caroline became pregnant again and Barbara was convinced that pushing a heavy pushchair everywhere was what led to Caroline's miscarriage. After that she was never able to have any more children.

It is impossible to know if Mary Ann was just a nasty piece of work or if she was a deeply unhappy and bitter woman who took out her discontent and resentment on those around her, namely her family. Whatever the cause, her behaviour propelled Helen in the opposite direction as a mother, one of strong love and selfless devotion to her children and grandchildren.

***

Helen used to read tarot cards and Ann told me about a time when she did a reading for the family and said, "Someone here is having a babby." She looked in the direction of Kristine, Ann's younger daughter and the oldest granddaughter present. Kristine shook her head, and it soon became apparent that it was Belinda, Linda's daughter, who was pregnant at the age of 17.

Ann told me about another family tarot card reading when Helen suddenly went white and packed the cards away. She and Linda were convinced that Helen foresaw her death in the cards, and she never gave any more tarot readings after that day. In one of her letters to Family Care, written around 1993, Helen said that she would be in Scotland for a few months as she had a job. Linda told me that she had a job in Glasgow working on a phone line giving psychic readings.

Over the years, Helen undertook several types of work. Tommy recalled her working in Gray Dunns factory in Glasgow and bringing home Blue Ribband biscuits; we always had a packet of Blue Ribbands in the cupboard in Stornoway, they were one of the most popular biscuits at the time along with Caramel Wafers. Later, Helen worked for Henry's who produced soft drinks and Billy told me the cupboards at home were full of Henry's bottles, almost lemonade on tap. She also worked as a bus conductor (known as clippies), at a car wash, and in various cleaning jobs. In both Glasgow and Australia, she worked hard over the years and always so she could help her family.

I found out that she loved reading like Ann and I, and listening to music, particularly Elvis Presley, Tom Jones, Shirley Bassey and Patsy Cline. She had an infectious laugh and there would be tears running down her face as she laughed at Billy Connolly's stories and jokes. She was an occasional social smoker, didn't drink much but loved singing at Christmas parties and one of her favourite renditions was 'Won't you come home, Bill Bailey'.

* * *

I have a lovely photo of Helen with Billy and Tommy, and I am guessing that she would have been in her late 40s or very early 50s.

Left to Right: Billy, Helen, Tommy.

Glenn and I had gone to Glasgow to meet up with Violet in Spring 2009 to learn more about Helen. While we were there, Violet gave me a portrait picture of Helen printed on a canvas frame twelve inches by ten inches. She was wearing a blue dress, and later Barbara gave me a photograph of Helen with Billy on her left and Tommy on her right which was the original uncut photograph. When I got home, I placed the canvas picture of Helen above the filing cabinet in my study. One day my friend and colleague, Eleanor, who had known me for many years, saw the photo and at first glance thought it was me. It was always the hair that created the impression that I looked like Helen.

* * *

Helen had suffered from breast cancer in the late 1980s and after removal of the tumour she seemed to recover well despite having no chemotherapy or radiotherapy. I wondered if that diagnosis had prompted her to go back to Glasgow to look for me twice in close succession. I learned that in February 1995 she started suffering from severe back pain and underwent tests in hospital. When Ann went to visit her, Helen said, "Do you want the good news or the bad news? The good news is that my breast cancer hasn't come back, but the bad news is that it's in my bones." I gather that Helen suffered severe pain in her final months. She, Sammy, and Stevie lived in a one-bedroomed house in William Street at the time and a month before she died, she and Sammy moved into a flat so that she would be more comfortable, and the situation would be less upsetting for Stevie who lived in the same house with his girlfriend. Just days before her death she wrote a letter to each of her children telling them how much she loved them and how she was so lucky to have been their mother. Barbara sent me a copy of the one she wrote to Billy, and I couldn't imagine the strength it must have taken for her to be able to sit and write those five letters. Billy found them in her bedside cabinet at the hospital after she passed away and gave them out to the others.

In her final few days, one of her children would sleep on a camp bed in Helen's room at the hospital so she would not be alone. The day before Helen passed, Mary Ann visited but seemed more concerned about herself than the fact that her daughter was dying, complaining that she wanted a cup of tea and a slice of bread and butter. Caroline and her husband, Sid, had brought her in her wheelchair and their son, who was only four or five years old at the time, was running around the room unchecked making a noise. Ann asked if Sid could take him home, which didn't go down well with Mary Ann or Caroline, and their lack of compassion for a daughter and sister astounded me. I was shocked but not surprised to hear that Mary Ann did not attend Helen's funeral and I wondered how on earth a mother could not even pay her final respects to her firstborn.

Chapter 19

Motherhood
March 1973–August 1974

After we were married, Mum offered us the opportunity of living with her at 157 Summergangs Road in Hull until we could save up enough money for a deposit on a home of our own, which was our ambition. In view of our previous relationship, it was a very kind offer. We accepted gladly because it would allow us to save more of Glenn's income, and the prospect of having to negotiate the steep staircase up to the flat in later pregnancy or with a babe in arms was not an attractive one. Also, there was nowhere downstairs in the Glencoe Street building to keep a pram, the same reason that Mum and Daddy had moved from their Torquil Terrace flat to the house on Kennedy Terrace when I was a baby.

The baby's expected delivery date was 12th March 1973, and everyone told us that first babies were usually late. Glenn had swapped his 'on call' dates for two weeks after that and his last on call day was 11th March.

I had been booked into Townend Maternity Home for the birth but two weeks before my expected delivery date the hospital laundry workers went on strike so they closed the home temporarily and I knew that I would now have to go to Hull Maternity Hospital on Hedon

Road which I was not happy about. Townend had seemed so cosy and intimate when I had gone there for a preparatory visit. In contrast, Hedon Road as the hospital was known locally was a sprawling monster with a poor reputation located next to Hull Prison.

I woke up on Sunday 11th March with a bit of back pain. It was around 8:30am and Glenn had just had a phone call from a doctor at the hospital and was dressing to go to the lab. I started to get griping pains in my stomach and told Glenn that I thought the baby was coming. He said that he had to go to the hospital to deal with this call, but he would ring round the other call technicians and get someone to take over from him as soon as possible.

After he left nothing happened for a while and I wondered if it was just Braxton Hicks. I waddled downstairs and had breakfast with Mum but when I went back upstairs the contractions started coming on a regular basis. I shouted to Mum who was still in her dressing gown that I needed to get to Hedon Road, and I rang the hospital number, and they asked me to come straight in. I called Glenn in Biochemistry and told him that Mum would take me to Hedon Road. He said that Mike Oaten was going to take over from him but he couldn't get in until 12:30pm at the earliest and that he would come straight to Hedon Road as soon as he knew Mike was on his way. We were not worried because we had been told that first babies can take a long time. As I was climbing into Mum's green Austin A40, which was parked outside her house, I experienced the strongest contraction yet and yelped. When she turned the ignition, nothing happened. She tried again but the engine did not turn. She started to panic but strangely I felt quite calm.

I asked her to try it again, but it was the same result, and I suggested that we call for a taxi. She tried one more time and amazingly the engine fired.

* * *

When we reached the hospital, it was chaotic with people moving around everywhere. After giving my details to the receptionist, a nurse or midwife or somebody took me into a room and asked me to undress and put on a gown. After what seemed like an age, a doctor and nurse came in and when the doctor examined me, he said that I should go to a delivery room straightaway. Someone shouted for a trolley, but I said I could walk.

A nurse told me it was too late for any form of analgesia but that I could have 'gas and air' which I knew was Entonox, a mixture of oxygen and nitrous oxide gas. I don't know why they didn't use its proper name, maybe because they didn't want to have to explain how it worked or simply that some staff thought that mummy brains couldn't manage anything that complicated even if they had some knowledge of chemistry. The next half hour or so was not pleasant, there seemed to be loads of people in the delivery room and they were all saying different things to me. The contractions became strong and although the Entonox helped it was still a painful process. I remember one person saying the head was crowning and I expected someone to tell me to pant but that didn't happen. I found the whole experience very confusing. Eventually my baby was born at around 1:20pm in the afternoon. The afterbirth followed, and I remember having an injection in my leg. When I asked why, a midwife told me it was to prevent haemorrhaging. Someone told me it was a girl and then took the baby and away, I didn't get chance to hold her immediately after the birth as I had expected. One moment the room seemed full of people and the next there was only me. The Entonox had made me feel lightheaded and a bit sleepy and it all seemed surreal, I wondered if I was still asleep and dreaming but I felt very sore.

A doctor returned and told me that I needed stitches and that he would come back later to deal with them. Why was there no baby? I was worried and asked where she was, he said she was fine and would be back soon. After what seemed like an age, they finally brought the baby back to me. She was very red, and her head seemed to come to a point. Then suddenly Glenn walked in, and I was so relieved to see him, I cried.

A nurse came in and washed my face, I didn't realise that she had soap on the flannel, and I spent the next 24 hours with a bright red rash because the skin on my face is extremely sensitive to soap. The nurse finally put her in my arms and Glenn sat beside me on the bed, she seemed tiny, although at seven pounds one and half ounces she was not small. Glenn joked about her head and said she looked like a baby police officer. The nurse said don't worry it was just from going through the birth canal and it would look normal very soon. I suddenly remembered that Mum was still outside waiting so Glenn went to tell her the good news.

Because of the laundry strike, doctors were discharging mums and babies the same day unless there were medical contraindications. Four hours later the doctor came back, and I thought the stitching was even worse than giving birth. Sometime later we were discharged, and Glenn took us home to Mum's house.

* * *

All the way though the pregnancy I was sure that I was having a girl, and I had chosen the name Katrina and planned to call her Katie when she was small. Glenn was okay with the name but said that if it turned out to be a boy, we should call him Cooper Steven so we could have a Cooper S in the family, after the car he was going to get one day. I was never sure if that was a joke or not and, in any event, it was a girl so Katrina it would be or so I thought.

Glenn went back to work a few days later and registered the baby's birth in the same building where we had been married just over three months earlier. When he came home from work that evening, he showed me the birth certificate and I was really annoyed. I found out that he had been talking to Keith Kemp, the chief technician, before he went to the registry office and Keith had asked if we were spelling Katrina the Scottish way like Robert Louis Stevenson's book *Catriona*. Glenn was intrigued by the idea and had registered her as Catriona. I was still sore, hormonal, and emotional, so I ended up crying for a long time when I found out that my Katrina was now Catriona. Mum had little sympathy and said, "Count your blessings, at least you have your baby." I felt stung by her remark at the time, but looking back now I can understand that having lost a newborn baby, the different spelling of a name seemed quite inconsequential to her. So, Katie became Trina. As I grew older, I started to like the lilting sound of Catriona pronounced phonetically as 'Cutreeunna' in Scotland, but if you live in England, which we did, the teachers, friends and pupils at school pronounced it Cat-reeona, which she hated so she decided she wanted to be called Tina, and Tina is has been ever since.

She was a good baby and breast feeding was easy although it did mean that Glenn couldn't take his turn to feed her. That was probably a good thing because he was still on call every 15 days, sometimes only managing two hours' sleep which meant he was tired for a few days afterwards. Very soon I was getting a decent night's sleep. I usually fed her around midnight, and she slept until between seven and eight o'clock in the morning. We adapted to being young parents, but we struggled around Mum who was fussy, tense and worried all the time about unimportant things. I accidentally broke one of her cups once and she made it seem like the end of the world. She was still very unhappy with her life but sadly I was too young and preoccupied with my own life to really notice, understand and be able to help her.

* * *

We were saving as much of Glenn's salary as we could and decided that we needed to find a house as soon as possible so we could be on our own. The competition amongst first time buyers was fierce at that time and we just missed out on several small, terraced houses on streets like Danube Road and Bristol Road just off Wold Road in West Hull, where we had decided we wanted to live. We should have been patient, but the pressure was mounting for us to move out of Mum's – not from her, but we wanted to be by ourselves. We finally found a house on a street off Willerby Road which ran parallel to Wold Road, and it was affordable although at the very top of our budget. It had belonged to an old lady, Mrs Goundrill, and although the location was good, we knew it would need extensive work and money to get it into a modernised state. No. 1 Woodlands Road was an end-terraced house with three bedrooms, a decent sized living room, a kitchen with a walk-in pantry and separate store cupboard and a downstairs bathroom. There was a dilapidated wooden green veranda attached to the rear of the house and it had a small, hedged garden to the front and a large severely neglected garden to the rear. We were so delighted when our mortgage application was approved, and we could finally become homeowners.

We moved into the house in early September and brought the sparse furnishings we had bought for the Glencoe Street flat out of storage. Uncle Ken had given us a combined stereo and television unit with sliding doors that he had replaced with more modern equipment, and we were grateful. We didn't have much money so instead of investing in an expensive aerial on the roof we bought a cheap internal aerial that only gave a decent picture when it was sellotaped to a particular point on the living room ceiling. Often Murphy's law would apply when a film reached a critical moment – the aerial would drop from the ceiling, and we would miss it.

Money was tight, and I can remember the week before Glenn's monthly pay day, often hiding in the recess under the stairs in the living room when I heard the clink of the milk float arriving on Friday morning, knowing that the milkman would knock on the door to collect the week's milk money. I always paid him two weeks money the following Friday after Glenn's pay day but I always felt guilty.

Glenn's parents, Marie and Jack, were incredibly helpful by either bringing us food or providing meals in their accommodation at the council-owned children's home on Wellesley Avenue in Hull where they had moved to as house parents shortly before Trina was born. I am not sure how we would have survived financially in those early years without their support.

* * *

Glenn was working on-call nights whenever he could to earn more money, luckily some of the technicians were happy to give nights away now and again and Glenn always snapped them up when offered. That brought more money in but not enough to make the progress on the house that we would have liked. It also meant that he was very tired because in those days before better terms and conditions of employment were negotiated, the on-call technician worked a normal day, was on call from 5:00pm that evening until 8:00am the following morning and was then expected to go back into the lab mid-morning and work the rest of the day. It also meant that he didn't have much time or energy to work on the house and Trina and I also had a broken night's sleep when his bleeper went off and he had to go into the lab. That used to happen several times on call nights.

As I child I feared the dark, I don't know why but Daddy and Mummy left the landing light on all night and my bedroom door wide open as a result. I always struggled to sleep when Glenn was out on-call and

I often went downstairs, put the lights on and dozed on the orangey-brown corner unit we had bought for the Glencoe Street flat so as not to disturb Trina.

We papered the bedroom walls with patterned anaglypta which was very fashionable at the time and painted over it with a cream emulsion paint, then we bought a brown shag pile carpet and plain brown curtains with a frill above to cover the bay window. We found an old-fashioned second-hand dressing table in Sellitt & Soon on Newland Avenue, sanded the varnish off and brought it down to bare wood. I found a replica old fashioned water jug and basin to sit on the stripped dressing table, and we picked up other items when we spotted something that took our fancy and was not expensive. Trina slept in our room in a wicker cot because we had not yet managed to decorate the second bedroom for her.

* * *

In December, when Trina was nine months old, I found out that I was pregnant again. Glenn always worried about money and was concerned about how we would manage financially with another baby.

We had a three-foot artificial Christmas tree when I was growing up in Stornoway with five sets of sparse branches sticking out at right-angles to the central spine, even ornaments and tinsel didn't do much to make it attractive. I decided that we needed a real tree for our first Christmas at Woodlands Road. Rose's greengrocer's shop was located in a bank of shops on the opposite side of Willerby Road, and they had some large Christmas trees displayed outside the shop, so I bought the cheapest eight-foot one they had. Getting it across the road with Trina in a pushchair was a challenge but luckily a kind gentleman passing gave me a hand. I propped it up in the small veranda, more of a 'lean-to' really at the back of the house and when Glenn arrived home, I proudly showed it to him. Let's just say that he was not as enthusiastic about it as I was, but two days later he eventually placed it in a tub of soil to keep it vertical and we went out to buy ornaments, lights, and tinsel. We dressed it that evening and I thought it looked magical if a bit lopsided. We decided to have our first Christmas dinner in our new home, despite Marie asking us round to Wellesley. I rose early and put the turkey in the oven, set the timer and went back to bed again. Three hours later, having opened our Christmas presents we started to prepare the potatoes, carrots, sprouts and made gravy out of gravy crystals and boiling water. When Glenn took the turkey out of the oven and opened the foil, we realised that I had cooked the turkey upside down. It looked a bit strange but tasted okay, at least I had removed the giblets.

* * *

Once we were through the cold dark months of January to March, the year passed quickly, and it was soon August. I was booked into Townend Maternity Home again and prayed that there would be no laundry strike this time. I had been a bit overwhelmed by Trina's delivery and decided that this time I would be more prepared. I read a lot about preparing for the birth and exercises I could do to help manage contraction pain. The baby's expected date of delivery was 18th August

1974, and this time Glenn swapped all his on-call dates that would fall between 10th August and 1st September to give us a bigger time window. His last on-call was Friday 9th August, and a doctor called him out around midnight. At around 3:30am I went to the toilet and on the way my waters broke. I called Glenn and he told me he had just reported the test results and could be home in less than 15 minutes. We knew that the technicians working on the Saturday morning would be in at 9:00am and they could run any urgent tests alongside the more routine ones.

That summer was unnaturally hot and being heavily pregnant I was extremely uncomfortable. Marie had come round earlier to take Trina out and when she came back and saw me struggling, she suggested that Trina slept over with them that evening so I could rest. Her timing was perfect.

Glenn came back as promised 15 minutes later and I rang Townend and told them I was in labour and on my way to them. We got there around 4:15am, Glenn helped me in and a midwife called Naomi met me and showed us into a single bedded room. The contractions had started by then, but they were not too frequent or painful. Glenn's bleeper went off about 30 minutes later so he had to leave and promised me he would get back as soon as possible. I was not too concerned because it looked as though the birth would be a few hours away. Naomi came in to see how I was doing, and after she had given me an enema and I had changed into my nightie, she sat and chatted to me because it seemed like a quiet night for baby deliveries. Stronger contractions started shortly after, and she advised me to put on a gown and get into bed. I told her that I was more comfortable in my nightie and would prefer to squat on the bed rather than lie in it as it was more comfortable. She was happy to let me do as I wanted and asked me to use the bell if anything changed. The contractions were coming about every five minutes and lasting about ten seconds, and I was counting and breathing out through them. The frequency increased to three minutes, and they were lasting longer so I rang the bell. She checked me and said that my cervix was almost fully dilated so it was time to put on the gown and go to the delivery room. The whole birthing process was so different from my experience with Trina. Naomi was the only person with me, and I could see a reflection of what was happening in the shiny metal surround of the light above the delivery bed. She told me when to push and I did; I saw the baby's head crown and she told me to pant and then I saw the baby being born. Delivering this baby had been a much easier experience, but both births had one thing in common – Glenn was not there! She was born around 6:45am and he arrived 20 minutes later. I was able to hold her immediately and although she seemed smaller than Trina had been, she weighed in at a healthy seven pounds, three ounces. I asked if I would need stitches and was so relieved to hear that I wouldn't.

* * *

Glenn stayed with us for a while, but he looked tired, so I suggested that he went home, caught up on some sleep and came back for afternoon visiting. He said that he would but first he would go to Wellesley to tell his parents and see Trina. Wellesley was a five-minute drive from Townend Maternity Home.

I was to stay overnight at the home and, if all went well, I would be able to go home the following day. Glenn came to see me during afternoon and evening visiting times and went to Wellesley to be with Trina in between.

The next morning, when I was changing the baby's nappy, I saw that there was a small cluster of yellow spots on the inside of her left thigh joint. The doctor on site thought she may have an infection and prescribed an oral antibiotic. Townend was a GP maternity home with a doctor on site, however, the decision about discharge was usually made by your own GP and Dr Bott, our GP, came to see me after his morning surgery. He advised me to stay in for another 24 hours so the baby's response to the antibiotic could be monitored. I knew Glenn would be at Wellesley waiting to know what time to collect us, so I called him there. Marie answered and I could hear Trina chattering in the background. I burst into tears as I asked to speak to Glenn to let him know that we could not go home with him that afternoon. He came to both visiting times that day and I was so happy to see him. My room was on the first floor, and I watched him walking down the long drive to the car park after afternoon visiting. The home had piped music playing and as I was watching him leave, 'When will I see you again' by the Three Degrees came on. Although it has an upbeat rhythm, the uncertainty of when their hearts would beat together struck a note with me in my heightened hormonal state and once again, I was in tears. Silly really because I knew I would see him during evening visiting.

The next morning, I was on tenterhooks when the resident doctor examined the baby and then ecstatic when he said that the antibiotics seemed to be working because the infection had reduced significantly. He thought it would be okay to discharge her so he contacted Dr Bott who said he could not get to the home that day, but he agreed with the recommendation to discharge us. Glenn came an hour later and took us to Wellesley Avenue.

I was dying to see Trina and when I walked into the large hallway at the children's home, she ran to me. She was wearing a dress with a green top and a green and white checked skirt and seemed so big at 17 months in comparison to the tiny baby I was holding. I knelt, hugged her with my free arm, kissed her and said something like, "This is your baby sister, and you are going to be such good friends. Will you give her a kiss and help me look after her?" Trina kissed her baby sister's cheek and held out her hand for me to take it in mine.

The baby did not yet have a name but after much discussion, Glenn and I agreed on Amanda Beverley. He wanted the name Beverley, but I wanted Amanda, which means 'deserving to be loved' and this time I got the name I wanted! We called her Mandy when she was little until, as an independently minded 13-year-old, she declared she was Amanda.

* * *

Tragically, the intransigence of her mother, Mary Ann, and the malevolence of fate colluded to deprive my birth mother, Helen, of ever being able to introduce me to Ann as her baby sister or being able to explain to both of us the circumstances leading to our enforced separation. A separation that lasted for 55 years.

Chapter 20

Family reunion, Melbourne
October 2009

Glenn had taken some persuading to make the long trip to Australia because he didn't like flying. He grudgingly suffered the four-hour holiday flights to Greece regularly, but a 23-hour journey comprised of a 14-hour flight between Heathrow and Singapore, a two-hour wait in Singapore and a seven-hour flight from Singapore to Melbourne was a vastly different situation. I had contacted a holiday company called Travel Bag to get some advice about airlines, flight times, visas, etc. Our travel consultant recommended Qantas airline, and we chose economy plus which gave us wider seats, footrests, and a dedicated purser for the cabin.

The flight was from Heathrow, so we travelled on the Intercity East Coast trainline to Kings Cross, from there a taxi to Paddington and then we took the Heathrow Express to the airport where we stayed overnight at the Sheraton Hotel. The next morning, we were up early and had breakfast in our room. Then we headed out to check in for our flight and explore Heathrow Airport.

The economy comfort cabin was bigger than I expected with three sets of two wide armchair-style seats in each row and plenty of leg space. We were offered a glass of champagne before the flight departed and I remember thinking 'this is the life'. I love flying and no matter how many flights I have taken, I still get that thrill when I feel gravity pressing me back in my seat as the plane accelerates down the runway and the upward thrust as it starts to climb up into the sky.

Shortly after take-off, the purser asked us to select our meals from the menu which we did and then settled down for the 14-hour flight. We talked about the flight and Australia, but I soon got drawn into my new Kathy Reichs book. Glenn started to read a fishing magazine he had bought from WH Smiths in Heathrow but as usual when travelling he was soon asleep, only waking up when our meals arrived. We had decided not to book the connecting flight from Singapore and waited for the next one some eight hours later. This allowed us to check into the Transit Hotel inside the airport and we had around five hours' sleep in a proper bed and a refreshing shower before the final leg of the journey to Melbourne. Changi Airport was huge, I had never seen anything like it, we even had to take a train to get to the hotel and we were still inside the airport. It was exceptionally clean, well signed and all the terminals had carpeting with no stains or litter anywhere.

The flight from Singapore to Melbourne took seven hours and on 3rd October 2009 we landed in Melbourne around 6:45am. We followed the signs to customs where we produced our passports with their electronic visas, and we were asked if we had any food or alcohol in our possession. Glenn laughingly said, "Wine gums," and to be fair the stern-looking security officer did smile.

Our suitcases seemed to take forever to appear on the baggage carousel and for the first time a bit of nervousness started to kick in. That surprised me because I had spent hours on the phone with Ann, Billy, and Tommy during the eight months since we had first contact, and I thought I knew them all quite well.

* * *

Eventually we walked out into Arrivals, and I scanned the crowds. I noticed Ann first standing behind the barrier with her crutches and we both waved. As soon as we had walked round the barrier and we were able to get to one another, we hugged each other tightly. Ann was smaller than I expected and very slim with straight dark brown bobbed hair and big brown eyes, very different colouring from me, and my half-sister, Linda, from the photographs I had seen. She was wearing a black reefer jacket, jeans, and a white polo necked

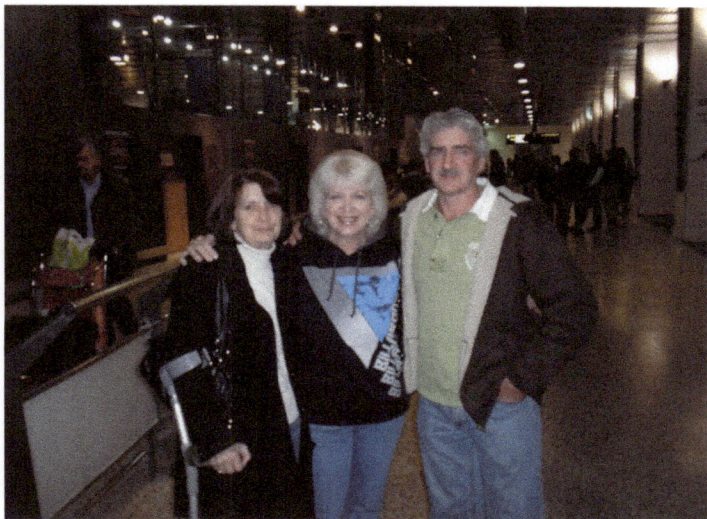

Ann, Me and Billy in the Arrivals Hall at Melbourne Airport.

jumper. Billy was standing beside her also in jeans with a pale green polo shirt with a white collar and a brown lined hooded leather jacket. Billy was taller, maybe five-foot-nine, had thick curly grey hair, a small grey moustache and his eyes were the same colour as mine, a sort of greenish grey. I pulled out my small Olympus Mju camera from my luggage and asked Glenn to take a photo of the three of us together.

We stopped for a coffee in Hudson's coffee shop inside the airport, Billy joked that it was not his although Hudson was his surname, and we chatted briefly about the journey and Helen before Billy drove us to Ann's house where we were staying. Ann said she was amazed how much I looked like Helen. I still couldn't really see the resemblance myself but all the family in Australia commented on it at some point during our visit, even though I now had shortish blond hair.

We left the multistorey airport car park and Billy drove us down long six-lane freeways, the land on either side was very flat and you could see for miles. As we got closer to the city, we could see the unique skyline of Melbourne appear with its undulating skyscrapers including the 92-storey Eureka Tower, which, at 297 metres, is one of the highest buildings in Australia, the distinctive Bourke Place standing at 254 metres and the Rialto Tower at 251 metres. There were many tall buildings under construction with huge red cranes hovering predator-like above them.

As we drove through more residential areas, two things struck me. Firstly, the houses were almost exclusively detached bungalows in contrast to the UK where two-storey houses are the norm and bungalows are in the minority. Secondly, Melbourne is in the state of Victoria and the British influence was very apparent in the number of buildings that had external decorative iron fretwork typical of English Victorian architecture.

* * *

Ann and John's house was a single storey detached house in Coburg, built in 1919. Unfortunately, John was not present in the house during our stay. He was in hospital following the latest in a series of operations on his leg, broken in many places after falling off a loading wagon on a very wet day some years before. We did get to meet him briefly while we were there by visiting him in the Royal Melbourne Hospital. He didn't look well, and it was obvious from his drawn facial expressions that he was in pain, but he was pleased to see us, and we were glad we were able to meet him while we were over there.

A short driveway led to the front door which was on the right-hand side of an open front porch containing two chairs with cushions. Inside there was a large area to the left containing a snooker table and two doors on the right which we later realised were the master bedroom and a separate bathroom. As we went through the door ahead, we saw a large open-plan area with a dining table in a recess on the left and a fitted white kitchen to the right with a breakfast bar separating the kitchen from the living area. Two steep steps took you up to the main living area containing a brown leather three-piece suite, coffee table and a 65-inch television sitting on a long unit. The floor had polished dark wood planks. Ann showed us into the bedroom we would use which was off to the left of the open-plan area. There was a large bathroom next door to the bedroom.

The house felt more like an apartment than a house and Ann told us that Billy had done the conversion for her. I knew that she had lost all sensation and the ability to move her legs, a consequence of an industrial accident five years after she returned to Australia. She had told me that she and John were working in a shoe factory and her job was to throw large bundles of leather from the storage area up to the operators on the machines. This caused problems with her spine and fragments of bone damaged her spinal cords. As Violet had said, she was initially in a wheelchair and her doctors told her she would never walk again. However, I soon realised what a strong and determined person Ann was so it was no surprise that she was able to overcome the medical opinion that she would always be in a wheelchair. I was amazed how easily she negotiated the steps and brought items like tea and coffee out of high cupboards despite being on crutches. She told me that she had had plenty of time to get familiar with using them.

After putting our cases and belongings in the bedroom, the four of us sat down and had another coffee. I was amazed to see that a book by Kathy Reichs sat on the lower shelf of the coffee table, the same book I had been reading on the plane. One of the many coincidences I encountered which to my mind supported the nature side of the 'nature versus nurture' argument.

Ann had arranged for the extended family to meet us at a barbeque in her back yard that afternoon and told us that it would last into the evening. We decided to rest for an hour or so to try to reduce the impact of jet lag.

During the afternoon, I met most of the extended family. There were 31 individuals in total, including my siblings, their spouses, their children, and grandchildren.

I had never been hugged so much. Before leaving home, I had created a family tree on paper and studied it closely on the final part of the journey to help me memorise all the names and who belonged to whom. I had packed light clothing but during the journey I started to wonder how warm it would be in Melbourne early in their springtime, so I bought a hooded sweatshirt top in Changi Airport and was wearing it when I arrived. When I was holding Nikayla, Ann's newest granddaughter, on my shoulder she was sick down my back, so I changed into another top. That worked out well because that October day at the start of the Australian spring became increasingly warmer and the new top was thinner than the Changi one.

My sister, Linda, was one of the first to arrive with her husband, Frank, and they had brought drinks and lots of food, including fresh prawns for the barbeque. She looked like her photos with a pretty face and a resemblance to Helen, the same colour eyes as Billy and shoulder length fair hair with a light auburn tinge. She came straight over to me and gave me a warm hug which lasted for ages, her accent was also Scottish but with an Australian emphasis on certain words from time to time. Her husband, Frank, worked in the Melbourne fish market, hence the prawns. He was not quite as tall as Billy, had blue eyes, grey-brown hair and bushy mutton chops obscured much of his face. He greeted me with, "Gidday mate, how ya going?" in a strong Australian accent and a big hug. Linda's daughter, Belinda, her partner, Ian, and children, Aliya and Christopher, came a bit later. As Helen had seen in the tarot cards, Belinda had given birth to Aliyah at the age of 17. She and Ian stayed together, worked hard at school and later at college and they finally got married in 2009 a few weeks after we left. She had her 'kitchen tea' whilst we were there. Kitchen teas are like bridal showers where close friends and relatives of the bride-to-be meet for tea, champagne, and snacks. Linda brought some homemade cupcakes back to Ann's house for us all to share afterwards.

Belinda had blue eyes, long blond hair, a loud voice and laugh and seemed very Australian to me with her direct manner and I was interested in the fact that she worked in human resources like me. Later in the visit, we had an overnight stay at Tom and Sylvia's house and going through some old photos, Glenn and I were astounded by one of Linda looking down at Belinda who was a few months old, sitting on her knee. The picture could have been of me with Amanda as a baby. Linda and I both had long brownish wavy hair parted in the middle and both babies had short blond hair.

Belinda's partner, Ian, was of Filipino origin, and he had a very smiley face and calm manner. Aliya and Christopher had their father's dark hair, dark eyes, and lovely bronzed skin. We met Frankie, Linda's son later – he had dark hair and bright blue eyes and towered over Frank who was standing beside him. I remembered then that Frank's family were Dutch and all the Dutch people I had ever met were very tall, particularly the men.

Billy and Barbara arrived laden with food and drink, and I found out that day that Billy didn't drink alcohol and had not done so for years because of a promise he had made to Helen. Everyone who came brought food and/or drinks so on top of the huge amount that Ann brought out of her large American-style fridge and cupboards, it was clear that no one was going to die of starvation that day. Barbara was around five feet tall, had blue eyes and a thick brown bob with lighter highlights. Although her family had migrated from Manchester in the late 1960s, it was noticeable that whereas Billy had retained his Scottish accent, Barbara had a full-on Aussie twang. We met Billy and Barbara's elder son, William, who was married to Carol and their daughter, Illaura. I found it interesting how the family name William had been passed down through the generations, so it was not really a surprise when I met his brother, Ryan, and found out that his eldest son was called Liam, the Irish version of William. Ryan had another son, Blake, and a daughter, Ava. I had brought some toy London buses as gifts for the boys and little teddy bears sitting in miniature Harrod's shopping bags for the girls.

We chatted to Ann's daughters for a while. Karen, her eldest, was accompanied by her husband, Alex, whose family had migrated from Macedonia, her daughter Chelsea, and milk-upchucking Nikayla. Kristine, the younger daughter, was there with her partner, Tony, who was from Sunderland. She had come over to England to work in her 20s, met Tony when they worked in the same company in London and when Kristine decided to return to Australia, Tony went too. Both the girls were shorter than Ann; Karen had dark hair with a fringe and brown eyes whereas Kristine had fairer hair and blue eyes. I could still see a strong resemblance between Kristine and my daughter, Tina, even though they were no longer children.

Tommy and Sylvia arrived late afternoon. In the photo I had of him with Helen and Billy, he had a thick head of curly dark brown hair and a brown moustache, when I met Tommy in the flesh, he had a shaven head and no facial hair. He was about an inch shorter than Billy and had brown eyes. Sylvia was a similar height to Barbara, had very dark hair, brown eyes and had a strong New Zealand accent. Tommy, who was a prison officer, sounded the most Australian of my siblings describing himself as a 'jai-la', not a hint of a Scottish accent to be found. I can't remember if we met their son, Kurt, his partner, Sam, and their little boy, Seth (nicknamed the Terror by Tommy), the same day or at a later gathering at Billy's house, there were so many of them. We met Amy, their daughter, who was a hairdresser when we stayed over at Tommy's house.

I had been made aware quite early that trades ran in the family. Billy was a bricklayer, Tommy had been a plumber and managed a plumbing business before becoming a gaoler at a high security prison in Melbourne, Billy's son was a plumber and Ryan was a carpenter. Tommy's son, Kurt, was also a plumber.

I looked around at all my newly found relatives and marvelled. I had seen dozens of photographs of members of my birth family at various stages of their lives but only in two dimensions. Now I was watching and touching them in the flesh and seeing the fully rounded characters that they were. Mum had died when I was 31, so Glenn, the girls and my in-laws had been the only family I had for 24 years. Now I belonged to this wonderful and welcoming 'tribe', as Billy called them.

***

The family had planned a series of treats and outings for us, and Billy did a great Uncle Ken impression by ferrying us around everywhere while we were on holiday so we could see the real Melbourne and nearby cities in the state of Victoria. We visited the Ballarat Wildlife Park where we were able to walk around and feed small grey kangaroos by hand; they put their little paws very gently on the side of your hand and nibbled the food provided by the park. Some of the kangaroos were carrying little joeys in their pouches. I had not realised that in addition to the kangaroos there were a few free wandering emus, and I found out when I turned round to say something to Glenn and saw one behind him. I squealed and ran to hide behind Billy because I have a bird and feather phobia. I could never recall any kind of incident that may have triggered my fear of birds so when both Ann and Linda told me that Helen had a similar phobia, I speculated that it may have been an inherited phobia as opposed to an incident-induced one. At the park, Tommy paid for Glenn and me to have our photo taken with a cute koala bear called Minky. He was sitting on a branch nonchalantly chewing a eucalyptus leaf and we stood either side of him. We were advised not to touch him because in some parts of Australia up to 90% of koala bears have Chlamydia, a sexually transmitted disease.

From the wildlife park we went on to the Sovereign Hill Mining Town which is also in Ballarat. It's an open-air museum depicting Ballarat ten years after gold was discovered there in 1851 and attracted settlers from all over the world. The main street is a reconstruction of the growing town and has hotels, a bank, post office, stables with farriers, bakers, grocer, a blacksmith and many other shops and trades. It had 250 volunteers and 350 staff, many in costumes answering questions and posing for photographs with visitors, much like the Beamish living museum in County Durham. Behind the main street are period cottages and a school and we were fascinated to see what living there in the 1850s looked like. We bought and drank sarsaparilla in the grocers and afterwards went down for a guided tour of the dark mine on a special open-air tram.

Tom persuaded me to pan for gold in the river and we both crouched down scooping up silt and river water in our tin pans, swirling it round and round, hoping that some raw gold would separate out due to its heavier specific gravity. Unfortunately, we didn't find gold and become financially richer that day, but Glenn and I both felt enriched by the whole experience of spending the day together with my newly found family in the sun at Ballarat.

* * *

We visited Altona Memorial Park and bought bunches of flowers at the stall near the entrance. After we had all put flowers into the spiked grave flower vases and arranged them in the grass behind Helen's gravestone which lay flat on the ground like all the gravestones in the cemetery, Glenn, Billy, and Ann left me there for a time. I told Helen that I was desperately sorry that I had not tried to find her sooner and I thanked her for the letter trail that allowed me to find Ann, Billy, Tommy, and Linda. I reassured her that I was happy and that I was loved and looked after well as a child. I was grateful that she had brought up such a lovely family who were so welcoming and thoughtful and I promised her that I would come back to see them over and over because now I had found them, I didn't want to lose them again.

Kneeling in front of the grave of the woman who had given birth to me then lost me forever, was a very emotional episode in my life. I struggled to focus on the wording on her gravestone through my tears.

* * *

Glenn and I were overwhelmed when we found out that Billy and Barbara had arranged and paid to take us to Sydney for an overnight stay. Glenn and I, Ann, Billy and Barbara, Linda and Frank, Tom and Sylvia took the one-hour flight from Melbourne Airport to Sydney on 13th October and we spent the day exploring the city's attractions.

It was a sweltering day, and Billy bought a sun hat. He should have tried it on before buying because when he eventually put it on, it was about three times too big for his head. Naturally, we all had to take photos of him wearing it or maybe it was wearing him.

Sydney Harbour.
Left to right: Billy, Ann, me, Linda, Tommy.

I had often seen the Sydney Harbour Bridge and the Opera House on television, but it was only when you were physically there that you realised how close they are to each other. The iconic arched steel bridge that connects Sydney's central business area to the North Shore took eight years to build and was opened in 1932. It's an impressive 1,149 metres long, 49 metres wide and the highest point of the arch is 134 metres high. I was amazed to discover that it had eight lanes for traffic and two railway lines.

We were intrigued by the Sydney Opera House which had recently become a UNESCO 'world heritage site' and I was surprised to learn that the architect, Jorn Utzon, was inspired by a peeled orange to create the sail shapes of the roof. I always thought it was white but when you get close you realise that the tiles covering the full exterior of the building are a mottled beige colour. We walked around the outside before exploring the interior and discovered that it housed seven different venues, the largest able to hold 2,679 people. We were all sitting on the steps outside enjoying the sun when we realised that Linda was not with us. She appeared shortly afterwards beaming and holding a brown paper bag that she passed to me. Inside there was a Christmas ornament with a picture of the Opera House on it.

She said, "Just a wee keepsake to remind you." I thought that was so sweet of her.

That evening we took a boat across to a restaurant on Darling Harbour. However, when we arrived there, we had to go on a frantic search for a pharmacy because the combination of new shoes and scorching weather led to a huge blister on my heel which had burst and was making walking a jaw-clenching experience. Billy soon found a pharmacy and with a thick plaster on my heel I was able to enjoy the meal sitting at an outside table illuminated by glowing overhead lights in the warm but dark Sydney spring evening.

The next morning, we went on a sightseeing boat trip around Sydney Harbour with Captain Cook Cruises. We sat together on rows of benches on the deck in the sun listening to intermittent commentary coming over the microphone from the guide in the wheelhouse as we passed places of note. Glenn and I were impressed because Frank gave us a personal guided tour, explaining about everything we passed in advance of the guide's commentary. Glenn and I teased him that he must be working in the Melbourne fish market during the night and moonlighting as a Sydney Harbour guide during the day. We had snacks and drinks on board which led to a slight incident when Glenn threw bread to the circling seagulls. I squealed and ran inside the boat. Billy laughingly commented, "Glenn must have a death wish," after the seagulls had gone and I emerged from the sanctuary of the main cabin.

We had lunch in a hotel in the city centre and spent the afternoon exploring the city. We passed a shop with slot machines and Tommy went inside and emerged shortly after with cupped hands full of coins having hit a jackpot.

We took a large taxi back to Sydney Airport later that afternoon. Our luggage had passed through the scanners without incident, and we headed for passport control but when we got there Glenn realised that he couldn't find his passport. A few minutes of panic ensued, then I remembered that he had it in his hand as we came into the airport so maybe he had lost it at the scanners. Glenn and I went back there and spoke to a security guard. He had found the passport – phew!

* * *

There were many other treats including a three-course meal on the luxurious colonial tramcar restaurant with Ann and Linda while it took us on a tour of South Melbourne including St Kilda. Ann also took us to the Directors Suite, one of the two cinemas in Melbourne at that time where you could watch a film lying on full length recliners with a small table beside you. Before we went in, we arranged for snacks and drinks to be delivered to us at certain times. The film *Julie and Julia* starring Meryl Streep and Amy Adams was not that impressive, but the experience was. Unfortunately, I fell asleep at one point but was woken up when my cheese and biscuits and a glass of wine arrived. Falling asleep was probably less to do with the film than the fact that we had had a huge meal and a few glasses of wine in The English Pub in the shopping centre before we went to the cinema.

We had a full day and overnight stay in Tommy and Sylvia's home. During that time Tommy took us to Captain Cook's house and monument and the famous Melbourne Cricket Club (MCC). Glenn used to play cricket, so he was fascinated by the tour which included a talk by a Shane Warne hologram that was incredibly lifelike. On the tour we were told about the famous Ashes urn, which was originally a small perfume bottle, and contained the ashes of cricket stumps created as a joke after England lost to Australia at the Oval in 1882 and newspapers printed a mock obituary on the death of English cricket. England and Australia compete for the trophy each year during the Ashes series and before we left the MCC, Tommy bought Glenn a replica of the Ashes trophy from the MCC gift shop joking that he could 'take the Ashes back to England'.

During the day he also took us to Old Melbourne Gaol which had closed 85 years before our visit and became a museum. On the guided tour we learned that Ned Kelly and 132 other convicts were executed by hanging there between 1845 and 1924 and we explored some of the tiny, claustrophobic cells. There was an interactive session where were all given a sheet of paper with a name and offence written on it. I was called Nina, and my offence was DUI (driving under the influence), but I can't remember what name or offence Glenn was given. There were 12 of us and a prison officer led us into a dark holding cell with wooden benches placed against each wall and we were told to stand in a row and in turn to state our name and our offence. Once we had done that, we were told to sit. There was no light in the holding cell, and we could only see because of light coming from the corridor through the open doorway. So, when the prison officer left the room, we were plunged into total darkness and hearing her bang the door closed and lock it was unsettling for us, but probably had little effect on the hardened criminals brought to the prison in the past.

* * *

On another occasion, Billy took us to the Crowne Melbourne, a sprawling complex with three hotels, a spa, cinema, bars, restaurants, and a casino beside the south bank of the Yarra River. Glenn and I were staggered to see the size of the huge 24-hour casino and the sheer number of people playing roulette, poker, blackjack, or chancing their luck on the hundreds of slot machines, which Billy told us were called pokies in Australia. Billy liked to have a little go at the pokies from time to time and he played a few whilst we were there.

He also took us to the architecturally imposing orangey-gold Flinders Street Station, which sits on the corner of Flinders Street and Swanston Street. It was built in 1854 and is still in use and the colour of the building can vary depending on the time of the day and the light. Directly across from the station on the opposite corner of Flinders and Swanston Streets and in direct juxtaposition lies Federation Square which opened in 2002 and is described as 'a venue for arts, culture and public events on the edge of the Melbourne central business district' on its website. The design is contemporary and the irregular buildings around the square are made of metal, coloured stone, and glass. I was reminded of the controversy in Edinburgh when the ultra-modern Scottish Parliament Building was opened. Edinburgh residents either loved it or hated the design, there was no middle ground. According to Billy, Melburnians felt the same about Federation Square. To be frank, I found Fed Square, its everyday name, quite ugly compared to the dated elegance of the station opposite and other Victorian buildings on Swanston Street and although Billy liked the idea of having such a centre, he had the same opinion as me.

***

We went down to Harbour Town several times either for meals or simply to walk around and enjoy the view.

It had been opened the year before beside Melbourne Harbour and comprised shops, restaurants, and apartment blocks. Billy pointed out what looked like the bottom half of a large Ferris wheel which if fully constructed would have been similar in size to the London Eye. He explained that the 'Melbourne Star', as it was called, was to have been a key feature of Harbour Town designed to bring in many tourists but shortly after the opening, it had buckled due to structural defects and was undergoing a long and slow process of repair. The anticipated number of visitors had not materialised and some of the shop lots lay empty. A short walk from there was the harbour itself with many restaurants at ground level set against the stunning backdrop of high-rise luxury apartments, their glass windows and balconies glinting in the sun. Both Linda and I speculated how wonderful it would be to live in one, but both Frank and Glenn were very quick to shake their heads. Many boats were moored up, a hotchpotch of charters, restaurants and privately owned vessels in assorted colours and sizes. If you turned towards the city centre, you could see the top of the large 56,000-seat Melbourne Stadium which was built for Australian rules football but also housed many different Australian and international sporting events.

* * *

We did something with some, or all, of the family every day, including many meals. All the treats were wonderful and enhanced our experience of Melbourne and Australia but the best thing about them was being able to spend lots of time with my recently discovered brothers and sisters and really get to know them. The more time I spent with them, the more I realised how different they were in terms of their personalities.

Ann was sassy, opinionated, knew what she wanted and was extremely resilient. Her fight to get out of a wheelchair after her accident and determination to lead as normal a life as possible was a testament to her strength of character. She and her daughters had an extremely close relationship although they teased each other constantly.

Billy was a shrewd observer, had a good memory for facts, was extremely interested in history, a very dry sense of humour and did not particularly like being in the limelight but he was happy for Barbara to be. When any of the grandchildren were around, not just his but Ann's and Linda's as well, you could see that he loved children, and they loved him. Although Billy was my younger brother by just under two years, whenever we were together, I felt the underlying strength and support that I had always imagined a big brother would provide. I understood why the family called him 'Rock' but I also wondered if it had started as a joke because of his surname.

Linda was kind, thoughtful and easy to be around and it was clear that Frank adored her. During the year of getting to know my new family by phone and email, I had spent much more time talking to Ann, Billy, and Tommy, than I had with Linda. While we were over there, she spent as much time as she could with me, and we became remarkably close. In complete contrast to Ann, Linda was not confident or decisive. As a group we went to many restaurants while we were in Australia and watching Linda choose an item from the menu became a standing family joke. She would stare at the menu for ages then look round at us all and say, "What are yous all havin?" After we had told her she would stare at the menu again and then invariably select the same meal that either Ann or I had chosen.

Tommy was the most extrovert one in the family, he had a droll sense of humour and liked to tease; Tommy and Ann continually directed friendly insults at each other. He also had strong opinions on politics and the way the government was running the country which was something he and Glenn had in common. On Thursday evenings at home, Glenn religiously watched *Question Time* on the television where questions from the audience helped David Dimbleby put a panel of politicians on the spot, and Glenn was very vocal when he disagreed with something they said. Like Billy, Tommy had a good memory for facts and told us many stories about Helen, how she would babysit Kurt and Amy frequently and they would return to find that Helen had woken Amy up to eat chocolate and watch television while they were away. Whereas Billy did not drink alcohol at all, Tommy liked his blond beer. We saw slightly less of Tom and Sylvia than the others because they lived some way outside the city.

I was disappointed not to meet Stevie and find out what he was like. I had been told that he had some learning difficulties due to a difficult birth, but he was a big strong man and had been a heavyweight boxer. I googled him and found out that Steve Hudson had had 11 heavyweight bouts, winning three, drawing one and losing six. Linda told me that Helen didn't like to watch him fight because she didn't want to see him get hurt. At the time we were in Australia he was working as a fork-lift truck driver on the docks. I saw photos of him and was surprised to see that that he had bright red hair but apparently there was a redhead in each generation of the Blyth family. My siblings all thought that it would have been a huge shock for Stevie to meet me because of the resemblance and that they would need to prepare him over a longer period.

* * *

When I started planning the trip, I had envisaged staying in a hotel within easy reach of them all, but Ann swiped that idea away quickly by insisting that we stay with her. I was delighted that she wanted us there but initially I was a bit concerned about how comfortable Glenn would feel living in what he would see as a stranger's home. I did not have a good cook role model growing up, but Ann loved to cook and was especially happy preparing a full English fried breakfast, something Glenn loved but only really had when we stayed in a hotel. She quickly won him over and I remember Glenn sitting at Ann's breakfast bar in his blue tartan-like patterned pyjamas enjoying his breakfast.

Later she said, "The first few days you could see Glenn was just watching us all carefully, but we must have passed the test because then he relaxed and started to enjoy himself."

I thought that was a perfectly accurate description of my very cautious husband.

* * *

One evening, Ann, Linda and I were sitting together, and we spoke about our weddings. I showed them my black and white wedding photograph and explained that my dress was brown, and Glenn's suit was burgundy when Ann surprised me by saying that she had worn a brown dress when she and John were married in Manchester. Linda showed me a photograph of herself on her wedding day wearing a rust brown dress and a fur coat, I shared the fact that Glenn's mother had given me her fur coat to wear over my dress. It also transpired that we were all pregnant at the time; I was five and a half months, Linda was seven months, and Ann was three months pregnant. Unlike poor Helen, we were all able to marry the men we wanted to marry and raise our children together.

There was an interesting postscript to Ann's wedding, when 25 years later, her daughters arranged a surprise second wedding on their silver anniversary. They even chose the dress, and Ann showed me a lovely photograph of her and John standing on a bridge in a

John and Ann's Wedding Re-do surprise.

large garden, she wore a long white dress and a flower headdress and John looked smart in a dinner suit.

* * *

Australia is the land of the 'barbie' and we had a family barbeque at Billy's house towards the end of the visit and this time Glenn was an active participant. Our daughter, Manda, had bought him a traditional Australian hat as used by the early settlers, complete with dangling corks, for Father's Day and he had brought it with him. He wore it that day at Billy's house and I have a lovely photo of him cooking meat on the barbeque wearing

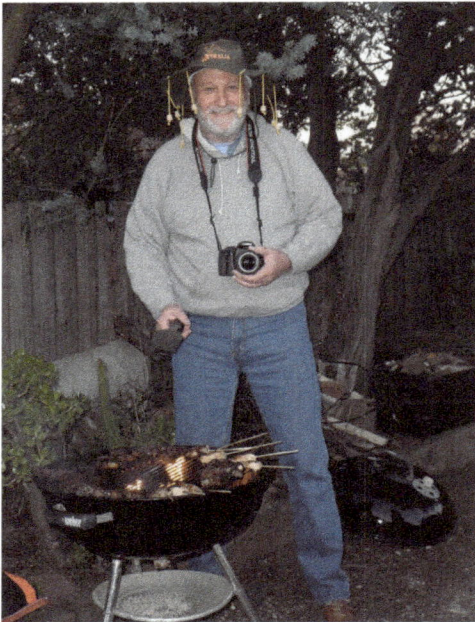

Glenn at the barbeque in Billy's back yard.

jeans, a grey sweatshirt with the habitual denim shirt and blue thermal vest peeping out at the neck, the Aussie hat, the colourful strap of his Canon Eos camera hanging round his neck, and he looks relaxed and has a great big smile on his face. The weather was quite mixed while we were over there, but I don't recall a day cold enough to justify thermal underwear!

Billy and Barbara pushed the boat out, the supply of food and drink seemed endless, and we had another enjoyable and memorable day with my extended family which stretched long into the night. Then Billy, our selfless chauffeur, drove us back to Ann's house which was at least a one-hour round trip for him.

* * *

Glenn had retired the month before our trip but as I was still working with limited vacation days, our visit was limited to 15 days in Australia plus travel time. Our time in Melbourne passed too quickly and sadly it was soon time for us to return home. I had brought gold lockets for Linda and Ann which I gave to them before I left and I was surprised when Ann gave me a gold locket, Linda gave me a gold locket and Billy and Barbara gave me a beautiful pair of gold earrings. In addition, they all gave us toys and gifts for our little granddaughter Lola, and we had to buy another small suitcase to be able to accommodate them. I had not known what to get for Billy and Tommy as I did not really know what they were interested in but later sent Billy a set of hand painted chess figures (based on key figures at the battle of Culloden) when I found out that he played chess and sent Tommy a silver pocket watch.

On 18th October 2009, our departure day, Kristine and Karen with her children, Chelsea and Nikayla, came to Ann's house to say goodbye to us. Shortly afterwards Billy and Barbara arrived and took us to Melbourne Airport where we met up with Linda, Frank, Tommy and Sylvia.

We had a snack together in the departure area while the clock clicked down too quickly to the time when the flight was scheduled to board and an announcement would tell us that we needed to go through to passport control and security. We all took lots of photographs and tried to put on brave faces but Linda, Ann, Barbara, and I were all struggling. Ann still smoked at that time and had to go out of the airport to a smoking area. While she was away, we heard the dreaded announcement. Thankfully,

Billy, Me, Ann, Linda and Tommy in the Departure Lounge at Melbourne Airport.

she returned quite soon, and we started to go through the painful process of hugging, kissing, and saying our goodbyes. I had made a commitment to return to see them again soon, and they all committed to coming over to the UK. I was in no doubt from the strength of the bond we had all formed that it would happen, and it did.

Linda, Ann, Barbara, and I were all in tears as we hugged, and I could see that dear Billy was not far away from it himself. As Glenn and I walked slowly and sadly down the passageway leading to the sliding doors that would take us through to passport control, I turned, waved and blew kisses through my tears until we could not see my wonderful newly found family anymore.

Eventually I composed myself and we set about following the standard airport procedures. On the way to the departure gate, we browsed in a souvenir shop and bought ourselves male and female Australian cricket shirts and a koala bear for Lola, my granddaughter, and one for myself.

As we were sitting at the departure gate, Glenn said, "Well, was it as good as you hoped it would be?"

I replied, "It was so much better than I ever imagined it could be."

* * *

From earlier chapters you know how my father's death and other circumstances made me reject organised religion and what happens after we die remains the biggest unanswered question ever. I just hope that if a part of Helen exists on some plane, she is at peace and somehow knows that I was finally reunited with the wonderful family she brought up and loved so much.

Acknowledgements

Thank you to everyone and the sources that helped me to create this memoir.

Specifically, thank you to members of my wonderful new family in Australia and Violet in Glasgow for all the photographs and information they gave me about their early lives and about Helen's life and character.

Also, thanks to my cousin Lesley for validating my memories of Grandma and Grandad Trowell.

Much of the information about Stornoway came from my memory and the Stornoway Historical Society.

Information about Australia came from Wikipedia, and I found historical details about the SS Australis on www.ssaustraliahomepage.co.uk and information about the Blyth's journey and arrival in Australia from Australia's National Archives.

"Ten Pound Poms" Australia's Invisible Migrants by A James Hammerton and Alistair Thomson (5 May 2005), Manchester University Press gave me a broad overview of postwar migration from Britain to Australia.

Thank you to Hamish Wilson at the Garsdale Retreat for giving me the confidence to start to write this book.

I am very grateful to Melanie Bartle at Grosvenor Publishing for steering me through the process of converting my draft manuscript into a finished book.

www.ingramcontent.com/pod-product-compliance
Ingram Content Group UK Ltd.
Pitfield, Milton Keynes, MK11 3LW, UK
UKHW051359020525
458000UK00010B/24/J

9 781836 151098